LEAVE
YOUR
HOUSE
IN
ORDER

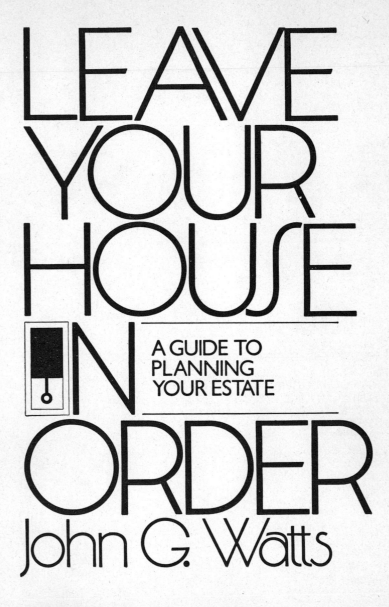

LEAVE YOUR HOUSE IN ORDER

A GUIDE TO PLANNING YOUR ESTATE

John G. Watts

TYNDALE HOUSE
PUBLISHERS, INC.
WHEATON, ILLINOIS

Scripture quotations are
taken from the King James
Version of the Bible,
unless otherwise noted.

Excerpt from *Three Out
of Four Wives,* copyright
© 1975 by Alfred Allan
Lewis and Barrie Berns,
is used by permission of
Macmillan Publishing Co.
Inc.

Quotation from *To Live
Again* by Catherine Mar-
shall, copyright © 1957,
is used by permission of
Chosen Books Publishing
Co., Ltd.

Quotation from *Widow*
by Lynn Caine, copy-
right © 1974, is used by
permission of William
Morrow & Co.

Excerpt from *You Can
Be Financially Free,*
copyright © 1976 by
George Fooshee, Jr., is
used by permission of
Fleming H. Revell Co.

Library of Congress
Catalog Card Number
79-66654. ISBN
0-8423-2152-7, paper.
Copyright © 1979
by John G. Watts.
All rights reserved.
Printed in the United
States of America.

Third printing, December 1982

This book is dedicated to my dear wife, Patty, who has been a constant source of encouragement and love, and to our three children, Bruce, Kathi, and Vicki, all of whom make life worth living. For them I leave my house in order.

CONTENTS

FOREWORD

It has been said that man will work more than forty years to accumulate assets, he will spend ten years conserving what he has accumulated, but will not take two hours to carefully plan for its distribution. *Leave Your House in Order* by John Watts has been written to help people distribute the property they accumulate during a lifetime.

If you want to know what can happen to your heirs when there is no plan for distribution of your assets after you die, read chapter 2 carefully. The problems and solutions are carefully and clearly laid on the line.

The basic document in any plan for distribution of property at death is the Last Will and Testament. John Watts tells how to plan your will, how to execute your will, how to use trusts, and how to assist your attorney in preparing the necessary "vehicles" for carrying your assets over the bridge of death to the person who will exchange his or her role as husband or wife to that of widow or widower.

Being a widow differs drastically from being a wife. It is a move from togetherness to aloneness ... at least for a while. It usually means a change in management roles. The wife who may have been a manager of family income becomes, as a widow, a manager of both income and principal. John tells in chapters 7 and 8 how to "teach your wife to be a widow."

In this book you will learn much about buying life insurance and what you need to know about death taxes.

John Watts is a planned giving consultant par excellence. His chapter on charitable estate planning is essential reading for any concerned Christian who wants to make a final gift to God in his plan of property distribution at death.

Don't miss Appendix 1, "Memo to My Wife." These pages of forms are worth the price of the book. Complete the forms, tear them out, and give them to your wife. Husbands would be helped a great deal if wives would complete the same forms for them.

I read this manuscript in about two hours. I learned much and enjoyed John's easy writing style. You may find the time spent in reading this book to be the best investment of time you will make this year. I recommend its careful reading.

Robert F. Sharpe, President
Robert F. Sharpe and Company, Inc.
Memphis, Tennessee

PREFACE

Recently my daughter Kathi was planning to drive to another state some 700 miles away. It would be her first long trip without my wife or me along to guide her. When she was very small I used to let her steer the car while sitting on my lap. When she grew older I let her drive around empty fields. I carefully instructed her when she got her learner's permit, and soon she was a very competent driver. It was inevitable that she would have to travel without me someday. I now called the auto club and had them map a clear, direct course for her trip. I made sure the car was in its best condition. We discussed how to react to a myriad of possible emergencies. She was well prepared for her trip, and it was a success. Because I love her very dearly I had prepared her as carefully as I knew how.

It is also inevitable that we will leave behind those who must follow a course through life without us. Are they prepared to do so? The greatest human crisis is death. Inwardly we avoid thinking about it and outwardly we avoid planning for it. Yet day in and day out death affects the future welfare of thousands of surviving families. The crisis comes to those left behind. *Leave Your House in Order* is dedicated to the courageous survivors who often walk an uncertain course buffeted by unfamiliar circumstances.

One of the greatest burdens to a family is the economic chaos created by someone's death. We can ease this burden by anticipating the financial consequences of death and planning a course of action aimed at alleviating the problems.

Having counseled many bewildered and uncertain loved ones left behind, I write this book with the sincere hope that the depth and commitment of your relationship to those you love the most will motivate you to leave your house in order.

As important as it is to plan for the welfare of loved ones left behind, it is of far greater importance to plan with certainty for your own future. The Apostle Peter sums it up best:

All honor to God, the God and Father of our Lord Jesus Christ; for it is his boundless mercy that has given us the privilege of being born again, so that we are now members of God's own family. Now we live in the hope of eternal life because Christ rose again from the dead. And God has reserved for his children the priceless gift of eternal life; it is kept in heaven for you, pure and undefiled, beyond the reach of change and decay. And God, in his mighty power, will make sure that you get there safely to receive it, because you are trusting him. It will be yours in that coming last day for all to see. So be truly glad! There is wonderful joy ahead, even though the going is rough for a while down here (1 Peter 1:3-6, The Living Bible).

The gift of eternal life is for those who trust in the living God before this life is ended.

John Watts

ACKNOWLEDGMENTS

Thanks to the many who prayed for and encouraged me to put in writing the ideas included in *Leave Your House in Order*. I am deeply grateful for your involvement.

Michael Tucker, pastor of Pulpit Rock Church of Colorado Springs, Colorado, first impressed me with the fact that so many lives are touched by the printed page. Thank you, Pastor Tucker.

Jerry White, regional director for The Navigators in Seattle, Washington, showed me how to plan and organize the material for the manuscript. Thank you, Jerry.

Phil Converse, vice-president of Robert F. Sharpe & Company in Memphis, Tennessee, attorney-at-law, and member of the American, Mississippi, and Tennessee Bar Associations, helped me make sure those special legal matters were worded accurately. Thank you, Phil.

Ed Summers, attorney-at-law with the firm of Caldwell & Toms, Los Angeles, California, and member of the American and California Bar Associations, made observations and suggestions enabling me to add vital items of information which have proved to be of great value. Thank you, Ed.

Betty Skinner, author and staff writer for The Navigators in Colorado Springs, Colorado, added the touch that made it all make sense and was a constant encouragement to me. Thank you, Betty.

Laurie Hopkins, my secretary, painstakingly typed all of the material. Without Laurie's able assistance it could not have been done. Thank you, Laurie.

Robert F. Sharpe, president of Robert F. Sharpe & Company, Inc., and friend of more than ten years, inspired me, through his enthusiasm for the whole area of planning, to pursue this part of my career. Thank you, Bob.

Finally, Rod Sargent, vice-president of The Navigators, my friend and closest personal associate for over twenty years, through his excellence of life and character has always provided the example I need for my life and ministry. Thank you, Rod.

ONE
THE ULTIMATE VICTORY

"Death is swallowed up in victory!" the Apostle Paul declared triumphantly, as he finished a description of what death means to the Christian (1 Corinthians 15:54, *The Living Bible*). How we thank God for this! Because Jesus Christ rose victorious over death and lives today, we share his spectacular victory. The ultimate victory is realized when a Christian departs from this body and enters the Savior's very presence. To be absent from the body is to be present with the Lord.

Mrs. Margaret Vermeer of Pella, Iowa, a few short months before she entered the presence of the Lord, told a group, "Most of us shy away from the thought of dying. We think there must be something wrong with someone who wants to talk about a morbid subject like death. The reason we feel this way is because America is a death-denying society. Death is a subject that is evaded and ignored by our youth-worshiping, progress-oriented society. It even shows up in our language. Instead of using the words 'she died,' we have many other ways of saying the same thing. We say, 'she passed away,' 'departed from this life,' 'went to glory,' or 'the patient expired.' We don't want to use the harsh words 'she died.' Yet death is the only thing that all of us have in common. We all will die. It's just a matter of time."

Dr. Paul S. Rees, editor-at-large with World Vision, said, "The time to die is now....Die now! It helps to get a lot of things settled. Then live forever!" Do now, says Dr. Rees, all the things you would want to do if you knew death was imminent; in fact, consider your death already past and start enjoying your forever-life now.

Think of yourself as a sojourning citizen. Heaven is our home. We are assigned here, as Paul described us, as ambassadors. Jesus assured us that he would prepare a permanent home for us: "In my Father's house are many mansions: if it were not so, I would have told you. I go to prepare a place for you" (John 14:2).

My associate Rod Sargent, vice-president of The Navigators, said, "To Paul, life and death are two great blessings. Death is good because it ushers him into the presence of Christ . . . to begin a life wonderful beyond human imagination. Life is also good because it is full of opportunities to serve Christ . . . to glorify him and to complete his work in this world."

For to me life is Christ, and death gain; but what if my living on in the body may serve some good purpose? Which then am I to choose? I cannot tell, I am torn two ways: what I should like is to depart and be with Christ; that is better by far; but for your sake there is greater need for me to stay on in the body (Philippians 1:21-24, New English Bible).

Our sojourning here is meant to be filled with purpose, fulfillment, and victory. We are created for his glory, to honor our great God and serve him. "You saw me before I was born and scheduled each day of my life before I began to breathe. Every day was recorded in your Book!" (Psalm 139:16, *The Living Bible*).

Jesus Christ and the people around us are life's most important concerns, because when we finish our assignment here on earth we will spend all eternity with Jesus and with people.

We love and follow Jesus Christ. By spending time day by day in fellowship with him in his Word and prayer, we gain greater insight into our mission here and begin to anticipate what he has in store for us when we see him face to face, As we love and serve our Savior, people become vitally important to us because we see how important they are to him. Paul told the Ephesian believers, "It is God himself who has made us what we are and given us new lives from Christ Jesus; and long ages ago he planned that we should spend these lives in helping others" (Ephesians 2:10, *The Living Bible*). And he wrote to those in Thessalonica, "For what is our hope, or joy, or crown of rejoicing? Are not even ye in the presence of our Lord Jesus Christ at his coming?" (1 Thessalonians 2:19).

People are the object of the Great Commission. We reach and disciple people—our hope and joy and crown of rejoicing. For all of us, it is a matter of introducing the people in our lives to Jesus, enabling them to identify with the Savior, helping them to grow through God's Word, leading them by our example to display the fruit of the Spirit, and then encouraging them in turn to actively influence others to follow Jesus. It is spiritual reproduction. The result is people. People who will inherit the kingdom of heaven alongside us. People with whom we will live an eternal life with a purpose. Life worth living! Then it is on to the mansion he has prepared for us when we step out of these bodies and into his presence.

But not so fast! You never move into one home until you clean up the one you left behind. I remember the day we moved out of 149 Via Guyuba in Monterey, California. We had cleaned the walls, washed the windows, waxed the floors with great thoroughness. The house was immaculate. There would be others coming soon to occupy that home, and they would have to adjust to a new neighborhood, schools, city, climate, and culture. If they found the home in as nearly perfect condition as possible, the other adjustments would probably be easier for them.

In a sense this was what Isaiah had in mind when he said that Hezekiah was sick unto death. Isaiah said to Hezekiah, "Thus saith the Lord, Set thine house in order; for thou shalt die, and not live" (2 Kings 20:1). During our earthly sojourn God gives us the joy of meaningful relationships, first with him and then with people. With some people—loved ones—we have special, unique relationships. Paul warns Timothy, "But anyone who won't care for his own relatives when they need help, especially those living in his own family, has no right to say he is a Christian. Such a person is worse than the heathen" (1 Timothy 5:8, *The Living Bible*).

Relatives and loved ones need our personal care and concern. We are moving on and leaving some special people behind. How will our departure, gradual or sudden, affect those we leave behind? Is our house in order?

No one likes to see loved ones leave. Recently Patty, Vicki (our youngest), and I stood at the end of a concourse at Denver's Stapleton Field and watched as Bruce's California-bound 747 rumbled down the runway. Soon it was pointed upward and quickly entered the low clouds of that snowy day. He was gone. We stood there for a moment, amazed at how quickly he left us. It takes special grace to leave loved ones . . . but wait, it takes more grace to put our lives together again after they have gone! We have the opportunity to make the orderly and God-honoring adjustment for those we leave behind—be they wife, husband, children, parents, or other loved ones.

It is easy to resist planning for something we do not want to happen. We do not want to leave the loved ones God has given us, so we avoid planning for that possibility. But part of our calling is planning our departure in a way that has a concern for those we leave behind.

Of special concern are widows. In 1976 more than 87 percent of all widows under age sixty-five had loved ones living with them for whom they had a responsibility. In the same year nearly 11 million women in America were widows. Perhaps this is why Scripture devotes so much attention to caring for and ministering to widows. The loss of a husband as the head of a home doubles the wife's responsibility. And widowhood, then, becomes a major social, economic, and spiritual problem.

A widow's two main problems will be loneliness and financial need. Loneliness often comes because she lacks a feeling of significance to loved ones, the community, or God. "Who needs me?" she cries. "Where do I fit in now?"

Her financial need can be disastrous, often due to lack of realistic planning by her late husband. The median income of widowed heads of households in the United States in 1975 was $4,312! Consider the fact that 90 percent of the widows aged 35-44 had children under age eighteen living with them at the time. Lynn Caine in her book entitled *Widow* says, "My first problem was that Martin and I had never discussed money.... I never even knew how much money Martin earned or how much it took to run the household." Alfred Lewis in *Three Out of Four Wives* comments, "The man who has never told his wife exactly how much he is worth has never told her that he loves her!"

Or listen to Catherine Marshall tell of her frustration at making the adjustment to widowhood in her book entitled *To Live Again:* "In many ways, I was still a little girl. I had adored and leaned on my husband.

Like many a sheltered woman who has married young, I had never once figured out an income tax blank, had a car inspected, consulted a lawyer, or tried to read an insurance policy. Railroad timetables and plane schedules were enigmas to me. My household checking account rarely balanced. I had never invested any money; I had been driving a car for only three months. I would never even have considered braving a trip alone to New York.

"Now I was faced with all of these practical matters, plus many, many more.

"There was some insurance, but not enough. I had no idea where Peter John and I would live after we left the Manse. I was not trained to earn a living. I had married when my college diploma was warm from the dean's hand, before I had even earned a teacher's certificate.... The adjustment that faced me, therefore, posed a challenge in every way in which a woman can be challenged."

Why not "Die now!" as Dr. Rees expressed it? The victory is ours. We can face it. It's so much more thoughtful toward those we love. Yes, leave your house in order as an expression of the depth of your love for those you may someday leave behind.

TWO
THE PROBLEMS OF DYING WITHOUT A PLAN

For years I have heard my friend Bob Sharpe say, "The State has made your will!" That uncomfortable thought should help us ask, "What really would happen if I died without a plan for the disposition of the resources God has entrusted to me? Who would own them? How much would be left after taxes, administrative expenses, and legal fees to be used for loved ones? Who would care for our children if my wife and I died in a common accident?"

Catherine Marshall, suddenly thrown into unfamiliar circumstances by the death of her husband, the late U. S. Senate Chaplain, tells of her anguish in *To Live Again*. Peter Marshall had left no will. She writes, "It was necessary for me to appear in probate court to post an expensive bond and to be made administratrix of Peter's affairs. Everything thereafter came under the jurisdiction of the court. Not even funeral expenses, doctor, or hospital bills, nor ordinary household expenses could be paid until the court passed on them. . . . Then came the day when I had to reappear in probate court to be made Peter John's guardian. Since then I have been required to give a detailed financial accounting of my guardianship to the court each year. This will go on until my son becomes of age. Each year the account figures must be sworn before a notary public. Each year a fee must be paid to the Office of Register of Wills for the accounting."

Probably not every state would make the same stringent demands that Catherine Marshall's did. Requirements differ from state to state. However, there are certain basic laws which are common to many.

WHAT HAPPENS TO THE WIDOW?

Especially traumatic is what happens to the widow when a man dies without a will. Most states allow her from one-fifth to one-half of the estate, with the remainder going to the children. In some states one child may receive two-thirds of the estate and the widow one-third. In other states aged dependent parents may be unintentionally disinherited. In many states, when a man dies without surviving children the widow will have to share the estate with her husband's parents, brothers, sisters, nephews, and nieces.

We usually assume that wives will automatically get the whole estate, and that they will take care of the children. But the state cannot assume that. The courts *usually* appoint the mother the guardian. However, in some states she must furnish a bond and pay bond premiums. Then she must arrange permission to use funds from the children's share of the estate for their support. Each year an accounting will be required and she will have to explain this to the court. Since the court is not sure what the husband intended to be done, it safeguards the children against a possibly careless and irresponsible mother. The state considers the possibility that there are dishonest, selfish, and greedy people associated with your family.

HIGHER EXPENSES

Another problem encountered by the survivor of one who dies without a will is that taxes and expenses increase. One unscrupulous New England attorney recently said, "I am delighted to discover one of my clients died without a will. It gives me that much more work to do." The most expensive route to go home to be with the Lord is by way of intestacy (dying without a will).

As a result of the Tax Reform Act of 1976, fewer people are subject to federal estate tax liability. So, for many, the lack of a will may not affect their taxes. For others, the absence of a will can take a devastating toll on their estates.

The costs of simply administering a will are far less than those of administering an estate where there is no will. In the latter case, everything must be researched, proven, and legally documented before final settlements can be made. Who are the real heirs? Where are they? Are there some who may not have been heard from in years? What and where is all the decedent's property? What is the extent of his debt? These and many more questions must be answered. A concerned and legally responsible administrator will take great care to determine the answers to those questions. He will not make any distribution to heirs until he is sure all liabilities have been uncovered and paid. This can be very time-consuming. Sometimes we think it is too expensive to make a will, but the cost is small compared to the cost of not having a will.

Frequently a bond is required of the administrator of an estate when no will exists. This is really an insurance policy to protect the estate. A bond would be unnecessary if the will names a competent, trusted executor and the bond is expressly waived in the will. An *administrator,* by the way, is the person who is appointed by a court to oversee the final estate matters. *Executor* is the term used for the person in that same position when he or she has been selected and named in the will.

In the new Uniform Probate Code adopted by more than fifteen states, the administrator/executor is referred to as a *personal representative*. The intent of this new code is to standardize the requirements for a will and to make uniform the procedures for administering a will in the states which have adopted the act.

COURT-APPOINTED ADMINISTRATOR

This brings us to another problem experienced by the person who does not have a will. The court appoints an administrator to settle the final affairs of the estate. He most likely would not have been the decedent's choice. Some very unfortunate things have happened when unqualified, disinterested third parties have been arbitrarily appointed to serve in this capacity.

Several years ago I was attending a Navigator function in the South. A young lady asked me what work I did with The Navigators. My answer prompted a story from her, followed by a question. She told how her father, who survived her mother, had died without a will. This young lady was her father's only heir. The court appointed an administrator to handle the final matters of the estate. He promised her that he would get right to it and it would be rather simple. But five years had passed! She had heard that these things take a long time and didn't want to bother him. He had never communicated with her again. Now she was through college and on the threshold of marriage. I introduced her to an attorney who was horrified to hear of her problem. Within two or three months he had the entire matter resolved. The original administrator, when asked about his procrastination, replied,

"Oh, it's here on my desk somewhere. I will be getting to it soon!"

I find that so often court-appointed administrators are too far removed and disinterested to give their personal attention to the victims of intestacy. There is so much benefit from personally selecting an executor who knows and loves the intended beneficiaries as human beings and shares their concerns about the future.

CONTROL AND DISPOSITION OF RESOURCES LOST

Perhaps the most devastating problem of not planning for your death is the loss of control your loved ones experience when everything is suddenly thrust into the hands of unknown managers who must follow the arbitrary formula set up by the state. By omitting a will from your planning, you lose the right to dispose of your property in the best interest of your family and loved ones. From that point on, everything will be decided for you.

Every family is unique, and every member possesses individual needs. Normally a state-made will cannot meet those needs. For example, a great many families have children who need special care or education to be equipped for taking their place in a productive life of serving the Lord. They need special planning and attention.

WHY MANY FAIL TO MAKE A WILL

Knowing that for lack of a will a wife may receive only a part of the estate, that children may inherit the greater portion at a time when they are too young to handle it, that taxes and expenses will be higher, that a bond may be required, that an administrator unfa-

miliar with the family needs may be appointed, and
that disposition and control will be forfeited, then why
do so many fail to plan ahead? Here are seven reasons I
believe most people do not finalize a plan. If these
obstacles are overcome, a plan will materialize.

A reluctance to face death. By avoiding the thought of
death, many people refuse to face its reality. "It can't
happen to me. It's too far removed." Then, suddenly,
death reaches our doorstep and its reality is clearly in
focus.

Some years ago an elderly lady in Florida had
refused to devise a plan for the disposition of her
property. Then someone very close to her died suddenly. Mrs. Ford observed her friend's close relatives as
they rushed to the scene. A battle ensued over the
unplanned distribution of her friend's estate. She
vowed this would not happen to her and called her
attorney. She was no longer reluctant to face death.
She understood its inevitable approach and planned
carefully for it.

Mrs. Ford told us that her estate was small and
would probably not be sufficient to see her through her
lifetime, let alone have something left to leave to the
Lord's work. She had no dependent loved ones. However, she had underestimated the growth of her stock,
which more than carried her through retirement.
Another very unexpected event occurred. Her sister
died and left Mrs. Ford a sizable estate. When Mrs.
Ford died, her estate, amounting to nearly a quarter of
a million dollars, went entirely to God's work. Her
initial reluctance had been overcome by the death of
her close friend and the tangled episode which followed.

Procrastination. "What's the hurry?" some say "I am
young and healthy. My father died when he was
eighty-six, my mother at ninety-two." This reasoning

often colors the thinking of younger people. King David recognized the brevity of life when he wrote that our days are as a shadow. Likewise, the Apostle James tagged life as "a vapour, that appeareth for a little time, and then vanisheth away." Because we think there is plenty of time we procrastinate. Like Scarlett O'Hara we say, "I'll think about that tomorrow."

One day in a lovely California community I sat with a friend and his attorney to begin planning the revision of my friend's will. The attorney began by announcing that his own will was hopelessly out of date and had been in his briefcase for months awaiting revision. What made him procrastinate? What makes anyone procrastinate? Simply a lack of urgency. My friend's attorney believed that the revision of his will could be put off a few weeks or months.

One event most likely to send one to his attorney's office to begin planning a will is a plane trip. Somehow air travel seems dangerous to many people and confronts them with the possibility of sudden death. Few people realize how incredibly safe they are, riding the jet-stream high above the many surface hazards of the earth.

We had just touched down at the giant Los Angeles International Airport when the flight attendant blissfully announced, "Welcome to Los Angeles and the termination of the safest portion of your trip. Please be careful as you begin your journey through Los Angeles." She knew all too well what we often forget—the safety of modern air travel compared to driving in Southern California.

The key, of course, is that we simply do not know the Lord's timing with respect to the concluding events in our life's work here. The safest and most considerate approach for those we love is to be prepared, to "set thine house in order."

Too little property. We look at what we own and say there is not enough there to matter. Some years ago in St. Paul, Minnesota, a widower died, leaving an estate valued at approximately $12,000. He died without a plan or any arrangements for the disposition of his modest estate. The State of Minnesota was obliged to go through certain legal steps to determine if heirs were living, how many there were, and where they lived. Over $8,000 was spent before the remaining $4,000 could be divided equally between the survivors. A simple, inexpensive will could have avoided this problem.

It is safe to say that modest estates need more thought and planning than larger ones. The beneficiaries of modest estates cannot afford to have squandered or wasted the small resources they inherit.

Another fact people often overlook is that the very cause of death may create an estate of more value than they realize.

The morning mail brought a letter from a university student in the West. He asked me to visit with him the next time I was in his town. Sometime later when I was there, we had dinner together. I learned his mother and father had died in an accident, resulting in a sizable insurance payment. He and his brother received a much larger estate than anyone had anticipated or planned for. An accident or ensuing lawsuit had not been part of the parent's thinking. And now these two sons had to assume a greater responsibility, since the estate was so much larger.

Suppose, for example, Mrs. Ford, our friend with the modest estate in Florida, had not finally taken the initiative to have a will prepared. The wealth that was subsequently bequeathed to her—money she did not expect to have—could have been lost in a mire of legal battles and disposed of in a manner wholly inconsistent with her intentions.

Too expensive. Many people feel a will is too costly. But it may be the bargain of a lifetime. Attorneys will gladly discuss their fees with you.

There are three kinds of wills. First there is a *noncupative will,* which is an oral will made by an individual usually during a last illness and under circumstances which make it impossible to draft a will in any other way. Witnesses are necessary, as well as certain other formalities and details attended to within a specific time following its completion. This kind of will is seldom used. There can be considerable legal problems, and in many states only a limited amount of property may be passed by this method.

A *holographic will* usually must be written entirely in the hand of the testator. Unwitnessed and dated, it is most often found among other valuable papers. It must meet other conditions peculiar to holographic wills. A recent check revealed that less than half the states recognize this type of will.

The will we most commonly use today is referred to as an *attested will,* so-called because it must be certified or witnessed. It must be drawn following certain prescribed guidelines which conform to the laws of the state in which the testator resides. Some states now subscribe to the new Uniform Probate Code, and so have identical standards. Other states retain their own distinctive standards for wills, though many of these are similar.

In each instance a will must conform to local law. Many people attempt to write their own wills, holographic or attested, only to overlook some large or small legal technicality. The result can be disastrous in that they totally fail to accomplish their purpose when the document is later declared invalid. Even when the document is declared valid, it still has created difficult legal work and expense for loved ones—a problem which could have been avoided with competent legal counsel.

One February morning I was reluctantly leaving one of those beautiful resort communities out West, where one dreams of spending the winter. The thought occurred to me that I had never asked my hosts, Tom and Edna, about their will. We had known one another for years, attended conferences together, and enjoyed many hours of Christian fellowship. I had helped them channel some generous gifts to the Lord's work. But I had failed to inquire about their will. I decided to do this on the spot, and found that indeed they had drawn a homemade version to express their intentions for over $1,000,000 in assets! I admonished them to get to their attorney quickly and make sure these vital matters were in order. I think most people take the do-it-yourself route simply to save money. It's not worth the risk. It may cost some money now, but it is incredible how much heartache can be created by the mess we leave our loved ones, plus the enormous costs which result from inadequately prepared documents.

Dislike for legal documents. How often we are afraid of the unknown. People are afraid of the dentist, the doctor, their first plane trip, a new restaurant, or a different route home. But lawyers and legal documents are awesome to the uninitiated. Some feel legal matters are a deep, dark cavern entered into only by the very wealthy or people in desperate straits. Besides, who can read all that legal tangle of impossible words, much less understand it!

I'll always remember a lady in Colorado who found it most difficult to make herself go to the attorney's office to have the document drafted. But when she did, everything went perfectly. Her will was prepared and mailed to her with instructions to review it and, if necessary, make any changes. No changes were required. She simply checked it, approved it, and put it away—unsigned. Some months later I was talking with her and she told me that she felt signing her will in the attorney's office with all the formalities was unnecessary. She simply did not want to go through any more legal mumbo jumbo. She declared, "Surely the judge will know these are my intentions. Why should I sign it?" Enough was enough, she thought, no more legal hassles. "They will understand," she reasoned.

"No they will not!" I retorted with equal adamancy. "Like it or not, you'd better recheck with your attorney and follow his advice to the letter, or all your effort will be to no avail." As I left her I hoped there would be a happy ending to her intentions to form a well-prepared plan for disposing of her resources.

Lack of ability to plan for the future. If ever we feel inadequate, we feel inadequate about planning for the future—especially in financial matters. The future involves thinking about death and retirement. No doubt these eventualities are implied in Paul's admonition to Timothy (1 Timothy 5:8) about providing for loved ones. We are responsible to provide during our later years too, when income may not be as adequate. Some serious planning at the right time will prepare us for that task. What would the economic results of my death be to my wife or other dependent loved ones? Chapter 8 deals with this in more detail, endeavoring to measure the adequacy of our present financial resources to meet the needs of our widow and dependents. This may lead us to consider changes which will improve the situation.

How have you planned the distribution of your resources so that they will reflect the best possible stewardship? The first thing to do is to evaluate your present position. You will find a detailed outline in chapter 6, "How to Help Your Attorney," because he needs to know the facts. What are the resources God has given me? Will those who are dependent on me have easy access to these resources? What if my wife and I die in a common accident? Then who will receive these assets, and how will they be managed or sold or reinvested? Will children have sole possession of our estate? Will it be in their best interest? Who will be responsible for these children as guardian? Should there be a trust? These questions and many more are considered in the chapters to follow. The future is never easy to plan for intelligently, but this does not make planning unnecessary. The very process of thinking about your property and what to do with it helps you evaluate your possessions and conserve and distribute them with greater understanding.

Reluctance to place confidence in others. Who will help put all of this together in a coherent plan? Whom can I trust?

One cold January morning I was called out of a meeting at Glen Eyrie, The Navigators' headquarters, to take a phone call. The voice on the other end was that of a familiar friend who said, "John, Dad is seriously ill. Could you recommend an internist?" My friend knew that I had visited a doctor specializing in internal medicine and that I had confidence in him. I gave her his home phone number with the assurance he would be available immediately to help. She called and he was. Frequently the best way to find any kind of specialist is to ask trusted friends who have employed their services and have been satisfied with the result.

Attorneys are specialists too. Many family medical needs can be met by consulting a general practitioner. Many family legal needs, including simple wills arranging for disposition of uncomplicated estate assets, can be handled by almost any attorney. But there are specialists who work almost exclusively in estate planning and distribution. With each passing year larger estates become more difficult to manage. The

Tax Reform Acts of 1969 and 1976 alone take a tax expert to interpret and apply to individual situations.

Deciding who can help and be trusted delays a good many people. It may well be that you will want to take several individuals into your confidence. At the very least, the key people who have counseled you throughout your lifetime should be consulted when it comes to disposing of your estate. Their part may be small, but their suggestions could be most helpful. These people may include the banker (particularly if you envision a large trust), the life insurance agent, stock and real estate investment advisors, and the development officer of one or more charitable organizations. Obviously, the key person is the attorney, who alone may give legal advice and design the final plan.

All of these people may not meet together in one place, but could be informed of the tentative plan and given opportunity to react with their suggestions.

Whatever the reason people use to forfeit their privilege and obligation to plan the disposition of their resources for the benefit of loved ones, it is not adequate or scriptural. Granted, Hezekiah was sick unto death when Isaiah came to him and said, "Thus saith the Lord, Set thine house in order; for thou shalt die and not live." But no one can really be sure of the Lord's timing. No one knows when he or she might be "sick unto death." Therefore, we must take Isaiah's admonition to heart and set our own house in order, now.

THREE
PLANNING YOUR WILL

There are three ways to distribute your property at death. First, *by law*. We have seen all too vividly in the preceding chapter how that works. Simply do nothing, and the state will make things happen for you.

Second, you may pass property to others at death *by contract*. For example, you make an agreement with the Mutual Insurance Company that you will pay them $300 a year if upon your death they will pay your beneficiary $10,000. That's a contract. When you die, your beneficiary simply presents the insurance policy and death certificate and collects.

Another form of contract would be a joint tenancy that has a rights-of-survivor arrangement. This is common in many forms of ownership today. It has both advantages and disadvantages. The survivor needs only the deed and death certificate to transfer the property from a joint ownership arrangement. The simplicity of joint ownership is thus an advantage. It avoids probate and related costs.

Frequently people view joint ownership as a substitute for a will, which it is not. There are four reasons why you cannot consider joint ownership as a substi-

tute for a will. First, it does not solve the dilemma
created by the coincidental death of both owners. In
such a case, neither survivor is alive to take possession
of the property. Second, it makes no provision for
guardianship of children. No will—no guardianship
planning. We'll come back to that later. Third, it
usually leaves the estate plan with no provision for
charitable giving. Finally, the survivor in a joint
ownership, no-will estate often stubbornly takes the
position that the decedent had: "Dad didn't have a will.
Why should I have one?" And so the problem of
disposition remains through another generation.

Here's something else to think about concerning
joint ownership. Enormous problems have resulted
from some spur-of-the-moment joint accounts opened
in banks and savings and loan institutions. Elderly
people sometimes open or change accounts to include a
younger anticipated survivor as a joint tenant. Sometimes it is not clear whether these accounts are intended to act in the place of a will or a convenience step
to give management freedom to a related associate.
Also, these accounts may conflict with the will and
create even more problems. An attorney may not have
been consulted about setting up the joint ownership, so
the conflict does not surface until the death of the
testator.

For example, Aunt Helen, age eighty, lives in a
mobile home and has a $25,000 savings account. These
are her only two assets. Her will, drawn years ago, says,
"I leave everything to my beloved brother Bob." In the
meantime she adds her niece Mary to her savings
account as a joint tenant and inadvertently has added
"with rights of survivor." Helen dies. The savings and
loan association awards Mary possession of the account. Brother Bob says, "Stop! Everything was to
come to me." There is a conflict and a battle ensues.
What did Aunt Helen intend to do? The courts have to

settle this kind of issue constantly. Coordination in all areas of one's estate is vital.

Still another dispositive device which is gaining popularity is the inter-vivos or living trust. This method has been useful in certain situations in helping to avoid probate costs, administrative expense, and delay in settlement. We'll talk about this in chapter 5.

The third way to transfer property at death is *by will.* One attorney accurately defines a will as "your direction in writing which most economically controls the disposition of your property at death."

Choosing your executor. Let's begin planning this will by deciding who should be responsible for carrying out your directions. Who will be your executor, or if she is a woman, executrix? The states which have adopted the Uniform Probate Code now refer to the executor as a personal representative. What will his responsibilities be?

After your death he must find your will and submit it to the proper court. First, the judge decides if the will is in fact the will of the decedent; second, he determines whether or not it was executed in accordance with legal requirements (including proper witnessing, etc.); and third, he figures out exactly what the words of the will mean—how the assets are to be distributed. The court then approves the executor, and it issues "letters testamentary," a legal document giving the executor authority to administer the estate.

The executor, authorized to be responsible for the estate, must first determine what is in the estate. This requires an inventory and appraisal of values. Sometimes assets are difficult to locate.

Some years ago a Virginia resident died. Everything seemed in order for the executor to settle a rather simple estate comprising land and securities, all in Virginia. One of the heirs recalled that the decedent, his father, had repeatedly talked about land he had purchased in Florida. No evidence was ever found of that transaction. The decedent, a widower, had not prepared an inventory of estate assets for the executor, which in this instance was a local law firm. An inventory is essential. This is discussed in detail in chapter 7.

State law requires that anyone to whom the decedent owed money be notified and that creditors file their claims within a certain time.

The executor must protect, manage, invest, and reinvest during this holding period. He must adequately insure estate assets according to their values. He must file returns where appropriate. (See chapter 10.) He must keep careful records, including the income and expenses of the estate. If a business is part of the estate, its unique management problems may complicate the executor's task. He must protect the business interests.

Personal property of a smaller but sometimes valuable nature may have been designated for certain heirs. The executor must deliver this property to them. He must collect life insurance that is payable to the estate.

The executor must take great care in making final distribution and accounting to the court. Obviously other duties may arise for the executor other than the ones discussed here. But this is enough to show the magnitude of his task.

What kind of person should assume these responsibilities? Most executors will be required to handle only a fraction of the potential list of duties because most estates do not require many complicated transactions. Where special expertise is needed, the executor will need to employ professional services. The role of executor might be described as a job coordinator. He is a supervisor who will get things done, for there will be many tasks which do not command the attention of a professional that the executor can do or get others to do. He must maintain the objective, press for results, and not procrastinate. A vital requirement for the executor should be empathy—a love, concern, and watchful eye over the decedent's loved ones. Business acumen is a definite advantage, along with good sense and sound judgment.

Who would fit this description? Normally a husband names his wife, and she in turn names him. This will be suitable for most situations. Sometimes, in the case of a woman who prefers not to deal with business transactions, a husband will name a bank as coexecutor with his wife. In other instances, an independent executor is named and the wife excluded. Too often the wife is not given credit for her ability to act in this capacity. Part of this may result from the husband's lack of communication with his wife in family financial matters.

Women have far more ability in financial matters than men are willing to admit! As an example, the primary problem in getting estates settled is simply procrastination. And men generally procrastinate more than women. So the wife cannot be overlooked as an effective coordinator for settling her husband's estate. One reason often given for excluding the wife as executor is that she should not be troubled at a time of bereavement. Consider this, however. The very fact that she is needed and has a task before her for which she is responsible tends to ease her grief. The widow who has everything done for her is consequently free just to sit and think about her loss.

I stepped off the plane in the beautiful city of Santa Barbara, California, one day and was met by a widow in her eighties. Early that morning she had lost her lifelong companion. She was still in a state of shock. On the way to her home I said, "Do you realize how much your family needs you? Do you realize how much your students need you?" (She is an art teacher.) She was also the executrix of her husband's estate. It wasn't complicated—a home with no mortgage, a generous amount in certificates of deposit, some savings, checking, and a small amount of personal property. Within six weeks she had resumed her art classes, the estate matters were well on their way to being settled, and the widow had paid two out-of-state visits to her children. As the months passed, I noted that she was busier than ever. She had clarified the goals of her estate planning, begun writing a book, pursued her art classes more vigorously, and had adjusted beautifully—all at the age of eighty two. I think she is a remarkable person. She is my mother.

The executor, then, needs to be a person who has empathy and good judgment and is willing to get things done. If the husband names his wife and she names him, an alternate should be named who will act in the event both husband and wife die in a common accident. The choice of an alternate should be made with these same qualities in mind. Obviously the person should be contacted and his permission secured.

An executor is not required by law to assume that responsibility; he may decline it. However, once the court has approved an executor and he accepts responsibility, then the demands are clear and he is required to follow guidelines set down by the state. He is required to act prudently and responsibly; if he does not, he may be held personally liable for losses which the estate suffers as the result of his failure so to act. He would not, of course, be held responsible for unavoidable losses.

It is often wise to name a close friend as an alternate, someone younger with business ability, who lives in the same state as the testator. Some states either require residency or make it so difficult for an out-of-state executor to act, that an administrator is named by the court to corepresent the estate within the decedent's state of residence.

Frequently the family attorney, if he meets the above criteria, will be named as an alternate. Still another choice has been the family bank. A corporation seldom has the kind of empathy an individual has, but an advantage is that a corporation seldom dies! Thus the bank is often used as the second or third alternate if more than one alternate is named.

Another important factor in choosing the executor of a will is to review the need for a bond. A bond is in essence an insurance policy guarding the estate against loss. Normally, where a trusted, competent friend is named as executor, the bond is not needed and its expense may be avoided.

The executor should be compensated for his effort. Quite commonly, in the case of a loved one with a small estate, the executor waives his fee in order to preserve as much of the value as possible for survivors. In many states the executor's fee is fixed by law. For example, in one state an executor may be paid 7 percent of the first $1,000, 4 percent of the next $9,000, 3 percent of the next $40,000, 2 percent of the next $100,000, and so on. In other states the fee is at the discretion of the court, a fact which makes me very uncomfortable.

In recent years I watched an estate being settled in the East, in a state which describes its fees as "reasonable and proper." No stated fee is prescribed. In this case the decedent's executor was unqualified to serve, so a court-appointed administrator was managing the distribution.* The estate was composed of two assets— a fifty-acre parcel of land and a block of mutual fund stock. The administrator sold the stock through a broker, to whom he paid a fee from the estate funds.

*Qualifying factors are discussed in chapter 4.

Then he transferred the land to a family trust in which he named the heirs the trustees. (In effect, he transferred to them the job of selling the land.) He had tax returns prepared with estate funds. He gave the task of distributing all the personal property to one of the decedent's daughters. For this task of parceling out the work and letting the estate and its heirs bear the burden, the court awarded the administrator $8,000! I shudder to think what that amounted to per hour for his meager efforts.

Finding a guardian. In most states you can name a guardian for your minor children, should both parents die simultaneously. This, of course, is a rare occurrence. However, guardianship should be included in planning.

What will you look for in a guardian? The guardian takes the place of a parent, and the court will usually qualify a nominee on that basis. Notice I use the word "nominee." Both the designated executor and guardian are, strictly speaking, nominees who must be approved by the court. Usually they are approved as requested in the will. However, the court is charged with protecting the estate against unwise choices and circumstances which may have changed since the will was executed.

A lady in the Southwest told me her executor had been an alcoholic. She asked if I thought the court would approve him. "No," I replied, "I don't think so if they were aware of his condition and if it affected his competence."

An attorney out west told of a young couple who named some friends as guardians of their children, then decided to name another couple as alternates. Subsequently the testators died in an accident. After deliberation, the court awarded the children to the alternates, feeling that their home was more stable and provided a better atmosphere for them. Observers who were close to the deceased couple said that originally the alternates had been a distant second choice, almost haphazardly selected. And although they were a fine family, they did not espouse the deceased parents' evangelical philosophy of the Christian life. You may find that incidents of this kind are rare, but I cite it to demonstrate the importance of extreme care in selecting alternates, whether as guardians or executors.

While I did not mention the problem of guardian selection as one of the reasons people fail to make wills, I do think it is a formidable cause of delay in asking the attorney to get started on the will. Admittedly, it is not an easy decision.

Let's discuss two necessary lines of communication in selecting a guardian. First, communicate with the children. If they are old enough, say twelve to fourteen, their opinions about a guardian should be seriously considered. They may have insights into the adults you have in mind that could alter your decision. Sometimes their observations about the children the prospective guardians already have may affect your decision. In some states children over fourteen are given a major voice in approving their guardian, even though they are still minors. So it may be wise to consider their opinion first.

Some years ago when we told our children about the couple we chose to be their guardians in the event of our death, our children were overjoyed! One of them remarked with a teasing twinkle in her eye, "I can't wait!"

Communication with grandparents is also necessary. They are often the children's natural guardians. They may not want the task, but I believe they expect the honor of being named and entrusted with the grandchildren. After all, don't they have a kind of right to the children who are part of their bloodline?

Some years ago a very young couple in the South named as guardians of their two children another young couple not related to them. Later the first couple was in an auto accident in which one parent died immediately and the other was not expected to live. Both sets of grandparents rushed in to find the will and prepare for their inevitable responsibility. They were shocked to discover that someone completely unknown to them was named guardian of *their grandchildren!* The tragedy might have been compounded, but mercifully the one parent survived the accident.

Some grandparents are beautifully suited to be parents again. Some are not. But in any case they should be consulted and informed of the reasons for or against their selection as guardians. Naturally, if they are selected you should ask their consent to serve before naming them. As grandparents they are entitled to know how and where they fit into your planning for their grandchildren.

What about financial resources to help in raising these children? How will the guardians gain access to these funds? Let's use an example. Mr and Mrs. Jones die, leaving two children—Mark, twelve, and Sally, ten. Mr. and Mrs. Brown are approved as guardians. Mark and Sally move in with the Browns. The Joneses' executor sells the Joneses' home and collects the proceeds along with those of Mr. Jones' life insurance, the only two assets. There are no taxes and the net proceeds after last expenses and creditors are paid come to $50,000, which will become Mark's and Sally's as soon as they reach majority. Meanwhile, if the Browns need funds to help with Mark's and Sally's expenses, they must petition the court for those funds. It can become awkward. Worst of all, Mark and Sally will become beneficiaries of a sum they are probably untrained to handle. This can be very detrimental to their development unless their guardians are gifted teachers and fit their role as guardians extremely well. There is an excellent alternative available called a testamentary trust, so named because it becomes part of the will and is initiated by the executor when both parents die and leave minors.*

Disposition of property. The beautiful part of planning a will is that the testator can seek God's will in all matters to be considered, rather than leave these important decisions to the state. The major decisions are who should receive the resources and who should be responsible for minor children. So our concerns are the ultimate disposition of the people and property God has entrusted to us. Since we belong to him and the resources are his, we need to seek his will about disposing of them.

The ultimate disposition brings these two elements together—the people and the property. Since people are more important than property, the first consideration is what will be in the best interests of the people. The answers to those questions are as diverse as the people themselves, for each person is unique.

A will enables you to provide for loved ones in the way you know they should be provided for. A wife can be given the authority she will need to support the family without court-imposed restrictions. Trusts can be used to provide adequately, but not excessively, for children. Timely dispositions can be made to the Lord's work. (See chapter 11.) Unusually dependent loved ones will need provisions in trust that, in some instances, provide lifetime resources because of their special needs.

I always enjoy the Northwest for its beauty and freshness. I think of a family who, in my mind, match the description of that region where they live. I have

*This kind of trust is discussed in detail in chapters 5 and 11.

visited their home on several occasions and have always been encouraged by them. Mr. and Mrs. Hudson are in their mid-forties and doing well financially. As a businessman Mr. Hudson earns an income that has lifted him to the 50 percent tax bracket. They have two children, Amy, fifteen, and Bill, thirteen. Bill has a learning disability which will probably preclude his holding a job that requires any degree of responsibility. In addition, his life expectancy is shortened by his medical condition.

Mr. Hudson's father just died, leaving little financial provision for Mr. Hudson's mother, who has come to live near her son. Her only income is a small Social Security check. Mr. Hudson wanted to provide $300-a-month additional income for his dependent mother.

The value of Mr. and Mrs. Hudson's assets is approximately $400,000. This includes their home valued at $75,000, holdings of common stock worth $225,000, and life insurance with a face value of $100,000.

A number of alternatives are open to the Hudsons in view of their circumstances. The least desirable of these would be to let the state do their planning. In their situation it is best to plan for the consequences of his death first, then consider the possibility of her dying first—something which is often overlooked. Then they should examine the possibility of their simultaneous death. Also, the possibility of the simultaneous death of Mr. and Mrs. Hudson and the children should be considered.

The first thing to note about the Hudsons is how young they are. God has thrust some unusual circumstances and resources into their lives. At their age and with the complexity of their financial situation, Mr. Hudson should find the most economical way to leave Mrs. Hudson with all of the assets and with as much flexibility as possible in managing them wisely. (More about this in chapter 7.) The reverse is really no different. Should Mrs. Hudson die before her husband, he would probably need all the resources too, as there could be some exorbitant expenses in the future.

A more complicated picture appears when we contemplate the deaths of both Mr. and Mrs. Hudson at the same time. A special kind of guardian will be required and a trust with some special provisions.* This trust may need to run a lengthy course to meet Bill's needs, while Amy's trust would have a different objective and termination point.

Now what if all four Hudsons should die together? Only one dependent loved one would remain, the mother, with an estate in excess of $400,000 before taxes and administration costs. Under these circumstances, one-half of the estate should be ample to leave in trust for the mother. The other half could be left entirely to worthy Christian organizations, including their church and its ministries. Eventually the assets left in trust to care for the elder Mrs. Hudson's needs could follow a similar course. The Hudsons have no other loved ones who have financial needs.

The remaining item of planning is how best to provide $300-a-month income for Mr. Hudson's mother now. Since Mr. Hudson is in the 50 percent tax bracket, he must earn two dollars for every dollar he is allowed to keep. Therefore, he would have to earn $7,200 to give his mother $3,600 a year. Instead, he designed a special short-term trust (ten years) for his mother. He transferred to this trust an adequate number of shares of stock to earn $3,600 annually. The trust began immediately and allowed Mrs. Hudson to receive the income without any taxes whatever. She did not earn enough to pay taxes, and Mr. Hudson lowered his income by the $3,600 and no more. While the stock is in

---

*The testamentary trust is explained in chapter 5.

trust, the dividends are considered to be his mother's income.

The Hudsons give generously to God's work and are careful about financial management. Their planning reflects good stewardship in the present and good investment for the future. I believe this is what Paul had in mind when he admonished Timothy about the serious need to care for the loved ones God has given.

Planning Economy. Perhaps the Hudson's adequately illustrate the economy of planning rather than letting the local law arbitrarily decide how to distribute the estate. The largest item to shrink an estate is debt, which can be enormous. Los Angeles County Superior Court Judge Jack Swink reported recently that the estate of the late movie actress Jayne Mansfield, estimated at $516,000, had been reduced by payments to creditors and administrators to an incredible $8,500! She left three children and no will!

Administrative costs usually amount to 5 to 10 percent of an estate, depending on its size and complexity. Considering administration, debts, and taxes, estates of up to $100,000 may shrink by as much as 25 percent, while larger estates may be reduced 30 to 40 percent.

The late Senator Robert F. Kerr of Oklahoma died possessing an outdated 1939 will, written in a way which was totally inadequate to meet his objectives. His estate was reported to be worth over $35 million. He had often spoken of wanting to leave a large share of his estate to charities, but had never documented his intention in a revised will. Several million additional dollars were paid in taxes by this default. God's work probably received only a fraction of what Senator Kerr intended to give. Most of us will not have a problem of that size, but that is a more compelling reason to economize by planning carefully.

One caution worth noting is that occasionally planners become so tax conscious that minimizing taxes becomes the priority to the exclusion of all else. This can become dangerous. By letting tax savings be first, you may lose the flexibility and versatility you need in providing for loved ones. It may sound strange, but sometimes it works to our advantage to pay taxes and administrative expenses.

Too often older Christians with small estates are urged to enter into irrevocable agreements with Christian organizations in order to eliminate taxes and administrative costs. This can in some cases be very detrimental. These irrevocable agreements do not permit the donor to reacquire the funds should they be needed. The agreement designates a certain income to the donor and this alone is available to him. In many of these instances the donors are placed in difficult circumstances that should have been avoided and which are not in their best interest. The economy of estate settlement must be balanced with flexibility to meet today's needs.

Personal satisfaction. Frequently people tell me how they have "put their house in order" and the feeling of peace it brings them to know the planning is done should God call one or all of their family home. I believe such prudence and foresight is honoring to God.

FOUR
EXECUTING AND
MANAGING YOUR WILL

After you prepare your will, you should be able to read and understand it! Many people say they cannot understand their wills. If they cannot, they should let their attorneys explain them. Some legal terms are totally foreign to anyone except an attorney. Ask him to explain them. Many attorneys rely on their secretarial staff to proofread wills, and some are not qualified to detect legal errors. Entire lines may have been omitted or key words and phrases left out, omissions that may be crucial in later application of the will. It is vital that a will be read, studied, and understood by the testator before signing. If a will cannot be interpreted correctly, the chances are diminished that the intentions of the testator will be carried out.

Once the will is understood, changes may need to be made. Ideally, all the details will have been communicated accurately the first time to the attorney. If everything is in order, the attorney normally will call the testators in for a formal witnessing ceremony in his office. This is important and should not be sidestepped by those in a hurry to get it done their way.

The witnessing ceremony. Some call their attorney just as they are going on a trip, announcing blithely that they are leaving for Europe and asking him to prepare documents leaving everything to the children and leaving the children to the neighbors. "Oh, by the way," they add, "we'll pick up the wills on the way to the airport and sign them in the terminal."

Haphazard for sure! Often the reasoning is that this will do it for now, and they can revise them when they get home.

How a will is witnessed can be crucial. Usually witnesses must sign in the presence of each other as well as the testator, and in most states they must be told they are witnessing a will.

Some years ago I was visiting a gentleman in the Midwest who was administrator for an estate. The testator, a friend of his, had suffered from an illness everyone knew was terminal. There had been time to do things correctly. A will was prepared, reviewed, and ready for signing. The man was too ill to go to the attorney's office, so the signing ceremony took place at home without the attorney present. Three neighbors were called in as witnesses. Not unlike many of our neighborhoods, they had not visited recently. They watched the testator sign. The first witness stepped forward, signed, then said to the testator's wife, "Oh, while I'm thinking of it, let me go right home and get you that recipe I intended to bring over." She left having seen the testator sign, but not having seen the other witnesses sign. In that state it was a requirement that each witness watch the other sign too.

The will was put away for safekeeping. Everyone was satisfied the matter had been handled properly. In a short time the testator died. The executor who was named in the will obtained it, called in the witnesses, and informed them that they would be required to appear in court to state that they had witnessed the testator's signature and had also watched one another sign. The recipe lady immediately told of her trek across the street and how she had not seen the other witnesses sign. The executor warned them that the judge might not accept the will as valid. Indeed he did not. The whole effort had been in vain. The will was declared invalid.

Most states require only two witnesses. However, it may be wise to have three in case the testator moves to a three-witness state, although normally that would not invalidate a will.

Witnesses need to know that they are witnessing a will but need not know the contents. There may be other informalities required by certain states which make it all the more important to let your attorney conduct the signing ceremony. If the testator is in poor health or very elderly or, especially, in a hospital, it may be important to have present, if not as a witness, someone with medical knowledge for purposes of establishing competency. This is expecially important if any kind of contest is anticipated.

Normally beneficiaries or representatives of charitable organizations who are named as beneficiaries should not witness a will. A pastor or staff member of a church named as recipient of some resources in the will should probably not be a witness. Younger individuals in good health are the best to witness. Not all witnesses will always be required to appear in person. Some may be required only to sign a deposition, that is, a witnessed written statement that he or she did witness the signatures.

Self-proved wills. Some states have now passed laws making a "self-proved" will valid. "Self-proved" means it is unnecessary for witnesses to appear except in special instances. This simplifies the court process.

In a self-proved will the statement preceding the signatures is written something like this:

We,_____,_____ and_____, the testator and the witnesses respectively, whose names are signed to the attached or foregoing instrument, being first duly sworn, do hereby declare to the undersigned authority that the testator signed and executed the instrument as his last will, and that he signed willingly and that he executed it as his free and voluntary act for the purposes therein expressed; and that each of the witnesses, in the presence and hearing of the testator, signed the will as witness and that to the best of his knowledge the testator was at that time eighteen years of age or older, of sound mind, and under no constraint or undue influence.

The signatures and subscribing statements then follow.

Safekeeping. When the will has been properly signed and witnessed, it should be kept in a safe place. It is also important to destroy any other wills which may exist.

The story is told of an eccentric old man who, growing insecure and somewhat fearful, placed his will in a most unusual hiding place—the rafters of his ceiling in the attic. When he died no one thought to look there! The only will that could be located was an old one which did not have many of the provisions in it that his family had heard him talk about. His attorney acknowledged that the old will was not the latest one; he even produced a copy of the current will. A copy, however, cannot usually be used in court as a valid will. Copies of other documents are valid, but traditionally only an original will is considered authentic. Even until recently, signed, witnessed copies were not valid. However, in two recent court cases, properly witnessed copies have been declared legally binding wills.

Most wills contain a statement in the beginning which revokes former wills and codicils or amendments. This is always a safe way to begin, as even an old holographic will may exist.*

One secure place is the safe deposit box in the bank or savings and loan association. Some argue that it is difficult to get to after someone dies, because state tax appraisers ask that boxes be locked until they personally inspect them. This can cause a problem for a few days, usually no longer. It has been suggested that a family having a great many items they usually deposit in a safe deposit box rent two boxes. One would be used by the husband and one by the wife. Mr. would put all his valuables and personal documents together with *his will in her box;* she, likewise, would put her items and *her will in his box.* If he dies, his box may be locked by the bank officials, but she can open hers and obtain his will and papers; if she dies, he finds all necessary papers in his box. This may not be practical for everyone. Some people now have safes installed in their homes. In the long run this may be less expensive and more accessible than a safe deposit box. Even so, a single safe deposit box may be used without fear of complications.

Attorneys usually offer to keep the wills in their fireproof office safes. This can be very convenient. But also, it may create a subtle imposition on the testator's survivor to use that attorney, in whose possession the will has been deposited, to handle the estate. There is, of course, no obligation to do so.

Review family changes. Let's consider some of the occasions for needing to review and change a will. First, there may be family situations making changes necessary. In many states births, deaths, marriages,

---

*A holographic will is written entirely in the hand of the testator himself and not witnessed.

and divorces invalidate a will or make changes essential.

This would be a good time to comment on the *codicil*. The codicil is an amendment to an existing will. It is important that a will be amended by the same process by which it was executed. A person might determine a change he wishes to make, then simply take a pen and scratch out the deletion and write in new wording. This will not work and usually invalidates the entire document. The reason is that anyone could read Aunt Martha's will, see that he was not to receive anything, and change her will to alter that result.

A codicil is a newly drafted section of the will, written to replace a section in which a change is to be made. The codicil is signed and witnessed with the same formalities used in the original document. Wills frequently have a number of valid codicils attached to them. They should be preserved in safekeeping with the will.

Family circumstances may also create situations which indicate that the will should be reviewed, amended, or completely revised. A common example is that of a couple, whom we will call Mr. and Mrs. Stephens. Their son Tim and his wife, Sally, have two children, Bruce, ten, and Kathi, six. Tim dies before his mother and father. The elder Stephenses' will states that in the event the primary heir (Tim) dies, his children will inherit his portion when they come of age. The result is that Sally has no inheritance upon the death of Tim's parents. This can be very awkward. She is having a difficult time financially and really could use the funds to help with the children. They cannot touch the fund until they are eighteen or twenty-one, depending on the state law. Part of the grandparents' reasoning may have been that Sally is not part of the immediate family and that she may remarry and give her second husband access to funds intended for the grandchildren. This reasoning may have some merit, but I cannot help feeling that leaving Sally out of the will creates two injustices: first, if Sally is a good mother and her deceased husband had confidence in her, so should Tim's parents; and second, it creates an estate for children too young to assume responsibility for it.

The death of a primary heir brings up another situation which occurs frequently and often creates family unrest. I can illustrate it by the provisions of a will I read recently in California. A widow surviving her husband had four children, and each of them had children. Her will read that her four children would share equally in her estate. One of her sons died, leaving his two children. Most wills read that the children of primary heirs will inherit "per stirpes" rather than "per capita." Let me explain this strange expression. A *per capita* distribution means that the property is distributed equally to individuals, while a *per stirpes* distribution means it is distributed equally to families.

Let's look at the California will mentioned above. Even though one son died, there are four families mentioned in her will to inherit her estate as follows:

Bill has 3 children
Vicki has 2 children
Arthur has 1 child
Bennett died, leaving 2 children

Let's say the estate value was $120,000. If the distribution is to be per stirpes, by family, here is what will happen. When the widow dies, her net estate of $120,000 will be distributed as follows:

Bill	$30,000
Vicki	30,000
Arthur	30,000
Bennett's child #1	15,000
child #2	15,000
	$120,000

If the distribution is per capita, it will be distributed this way:

Bill	$24,000
Vicki	24,000
Arthur	24,000
Bennett's child #1	24,000
child #2	24,000
	$120,000

You can see the effect in a clearer way, perhaps, by assuming no children survived the widow, only grandchildren:

Family	Per Stirpes (by family)		Per Capita (by individuals)	
Bill's 3 children	$10,000 /child	($30,000)	$15,000 /child	($45,000)
Vicki's 2 children	15,000 /child	(30,000)	15,000 /child	(30,000)
Arthur's 1 child	30,000	(30,000)	15,000	(15,000)
Bennett's 2 children	15,000 /child	(30,000)	15,000 /child	(30,000)
		$120,000		$120,000

The testator needs to consider carefully how he wants his estate distributed.

Executor change. Another crucial factor affecting wills is the need to change executors. An executor may move, affecting his suitability, or may be disqualified by virtue of the testator's move. We have discussed this earlier, but we should mention here the need to monitor and reassess the qualification of the executor. Often people review their wills, made up years ago, and discover that their executors have died or in some other way are disqualified. When Robert F. Kennedy was assassinated in Los Angeles, his brother John F. Kennedy had already died in Dallas. John was Robert's executor. No doubt an alternate had been nominated to serve if John had not survived Robert.

My father's executor was elected to Congress and under those circumstances was not qualified to serve. Election to public office frequently creates this problem. Other serious situations may arise, making it not advisable for the executor to serve. Loss of judgment, age, a handicap, additional responsibilities which raise doubt about his capacity to assume another job, all could mean a change is in order. You need to review and decide periodically.

Guardian changes. The same applies to the guardian. Is the couple you name still a good choice? One area of concern which arises in mission organizations like The Navigators is that a young couple names as guardian another couple who subsequently move to another country. They may or may not be legally able to become the children's guardians. Even if they could, would it be a good decision?

After a seminar I had conducted in Albuquerque, a missionary approached me and asked who in the world would take the children if they, the parents, would die. They had eleven! Who indeed? They would probably have to divide them among several families.

Review after a change of residence. Another occasion for question would be the testator's move to another state. It is probably a good rule of thumb to review your will whenever you move. I hope all fifty states will soon decide to accept the Uniform Probate Code, making laws concerning wills uniform in all states. Until then, wills should be reviewed from state to state. I am often asked by Navigator staff members going to work in another country in which state they should make their wills. I usually advise them to use the state where they are registered to vote. Another consideration is where they own real property. Each state holds a probate proceeding when the owner of real property dies leaving property to be distributed by will. This is called an ancillary probate. The attorney will know about all real property, its location, and the nature of the title. He can write the will to qualify in each state where a proceeding could take place.

Review when property changes. Still another reason to review a will is a change in the nature of the property, its values or income. I heard of a widower with two sons on the West Coast. One son showed special love for the family home where his father lived. So the father redrafted his will upon the death of his wife, leaving his home to that son and his cash and securities to the other. This represented a fairly equal settlement. But as the years passed, the father decided to sell his home and move into a retirement complex. He forgot to change his will and thus unintentionally disinherited one son.

Another man left $100,000, the major portion of his estate, to his wife and the rest to charity. He grew very rich, never changed his will, and the charities received over $10,000,000! This really amounts to disinheritance. There are complex rules from state to state giving husbands and wives certain rights to each other's estates. These rights cannot be taken away even by an otherwise valid will.

Review taxes. Changes in wills are more common today in view of tax reforms. The Tax Reform Acts of 1969 and 1976 caused enormous changes in estate planning, particularly the 1976 law. Chapter 10 of this book deals with how taxes affect your planning to leave your house in order. Generally the 1976 Act makes it possible for more estates to escape federal estate tax.

Review the distribution process. Managing a will means that one monitors his assets and how they would be disposed of at his death. A watchful eye is necessary in this matter because most people make a list of the resources they own, have a will drawn, then enter into a myriad of transactions that change or nullify its provisions. The will disposes of only those assets included in it. So it can happen that property is transferred entirely outside of probate without the will having had any effect.

An example of this might be a young couple with few or no assets—maybe a new home with a small equity at best, and life insurance by far their largest asset. When their baby is born, they make a will with a trust carefully designed to care for Junior's needs. Their life insurance names the wife primary beneficiary and Junior the secondary beneficiary. The couple dies in a common accident and Junior, via his guardian, inherits the insurance proceeds which bypass the will and the trust set up just for him, because the insurance was not designated to go to him through the trust.

Let's review what kind of property bypasses probate. Life insurance does if a beneficiary is living to receive it. Otherwise it will go through the will to the heirs named in the will.

Jointly owned property which has rights of survivorship will also bypass a court proceeding, providing that was the clear intent of the title. As we have seen, much controversy surrounds joint ownership because of the conflict it could produce with the will. Again, this is a management problem. The will is ignored, not referred to, and soon the process of distribution has developed a snag. In some states there is a similar title to property known as "tenancy by the entirety." This title, where it is recognized, is entered into only by husband and wife, but still accomplishes the same dispositive purpose as joint tenancy. Both normally bypass probate.

By contrast, "tenants in common" represents individual (undivided) interest of two or more owners. If John and Sally are married, own their home in a "tenants in common" arrangement, when John dies his interest must pass to Sally through his will. But if John and Sally had had a joint-tenancy arrangement, Sally would have bypassed the court proceeding and, presenting the deed and death certificate to appropriate officials, had a new deed drawn up in her name alone. There may be instances, however, when a tenants-in-common situation is advantageous, especially from a tax standpoint.

Review beneficiaries. Many are surprised to reread old wills and discover that intended beneficiaries have died. As a general rule, I believe that in view of a man's responsibility to provide for dependent loved ones, younger couples should leave their entire estates to each other. When there are children, the surviving parent's responsibility may be of a very long term. Serious consideration should be given to naming a contingent beneficiary in the event the young couple and their children all die in a common accident.

Scripturally, probably the first thought should be given to parents. Matthew 15:5, 6 in *The Living Bible* speaks to this issue:

"But you say, 'Even if your parents are in need, you may give their support money to the church instead.' And so, by your man-made rule, you nullify the direct command of God to honor and care for your parents."

A sailor at a Navigator conference down South told me that he had one asset, an insurance policy, in which The Navigators was the sole beneficiary. I thanked him for his thoughtfulness. I then inquired about his parents. His father could not work, so his mother was the only one working. Their financial future did not look promising—their income was low and the young sailor was helping them. I called his attention to Matthew 15:5, 6 and suggested he give his decision some serious thought and prayer.

Reviewing beneficiaries later in a marriage when the children are out of the nest, educated, raising their own families, and only mother and dad are left, considerations are different. Depending on the size of the estate, mother will probably leave everything to dad, and dad everything to mother. Upon their death, I believe generous gifts may be made to the Lord's work. The biblical responsibilities toward dependent loved ones have been carried out. There are differing opinions within the body of Christ about disposing of assets in this latter situation. Many Christians leave almost everything to their children, while others leave small remembrances to their children once they are grown and the major share to the work of God.

Review bequests. Bequests are usually designated in two ways—dollar bequests and percentage bequests. It is nearly always considered safer to indicate bequests in percentages. The owner of a prominent hotel in Chicago wrote a will in 1921 with specific dollar bequests to fine worthy charitable organizations and the rest to his wife and son. He died in 1933 leaving only $50,000. Had the estate paid his bequests and debts, there would have been nothing left for his wife and son. I am told that in this instance the charities placed all their bequests in a trust to provide for the widow, the remainder in the trust to be divided after her death by the charities. Actually, the widow could not have been deprived of her share. The percentage approach is always better.

Frequently a clause is used which disposes of the rest of the estate after certain percentages have been allotted to those the testator wishes to provide for. Harry Brown, a widower, might provide for two sisters by stating "one-half of my estate after expenses is to be shared equally by my sister Alice and my sister Bernice. The remainder is to be divided equally by [my church] and [my favorite mission agency]."

Managing a will is a continuous process reaching beyond the signing ceremony in the attorney's office. Your will should be scheduled for periodic review.

FIVE
WHO NEEDS A TRUST?

The simplest way to describe a trust is to say that it gives the benefits of property ownership without the burden of property management. Before discussing who needs a trust, let's look inside a trust to see what makes it tick.

A trust has to have five parts. First a *trustor*, the one who establishes a trust. One or more people decide they want to establish a trust and ask their attorney to write an agreement. By this agreement they will arrange to have someone else bear the burden of managing certain resources, while they or someone they appoint receive the benefit. The second part is the *trustee,* the person or entity willing to accept the responsibility of managing the trust for the benefit of someone else. Sometimes the trustor appoints himself as trustee—we shall see why in a moment. Sometimes the trustor appoints himself and someone else as trustee, or he simply appoints a bank to do this for him.

Next, we place something of value in the trust. These assets are called the *corpus*. It may be stocks, bonds, real estate, life insurance, or something else which suits the purpose of the trust. Then we have *benefici-*

aries, the person or persons who are to benefit from the trust now or sometime in the future. Finally there are *terms* or conditions which spell out the purpose and duration of the trust document. In summary, these are the five parts of a trust:

Trustor—creator of the trust
Trustee—manager of the trust
Corpus—assets in the trust
Beneficiaries—recipients of the benefits
Terms—conditions of the trust

There are two kinds of trusts. First, the *inter-vivos* trust, meaning "between the living," established now to meet an immediate purpose. These are commonly called living trusts. Second, the *testamentary* trust which is written into a will to become effective after the death of one or more people.

Let's begin with the *living trust*. Who needs a living trust?

Helen Waterman died a few short years ago at the age of ninety-two. Our family had known Helen for many years and often visited her. She spent almost her entire lifetime in New York City working for a physician. When she retired, he paid her a generous bonus which was added to her stock portfolio accumulated during years of frugal living. She had garnered a very adequate sum on which to retire. She never married. She was a thoughtful person and a consistent donor to God's work.

One day while visiting Helen I realized her memory was slipping. Her dividend checks were being misplaced, as were her Social Security checks. She was an ideal candidate for a trust. When I explained the concepts to her, she immediately recognized her need. She marched right to her bank and met with the trust officer, who in consultation with her attorney drafted a trust which would be in harmony with her will. Helen

Waterman, *trustor,* created the trust. A local bank acted as *trustee*. Helen was the sole *beneficiary* while she was living. The *corpus* consisted of stocks, bonds, and certificates of deposit. The *terms* stated that Helen would receive all of the income while she could manage to pay her own bills and handle her own checking account. This turned out to be a very short time. The bank then managed all her finances for her, doing so until she died some five years later. The trust was so written that Helen was entitled to withdraw any sums above and beyond the income, should the need arise, add more stock or appropriate corpus, change trustees, or revoke the agreement entirely. In essense, this revocable living trust had written into it maximum flexibility and yet accomplished her purposes beautifully.

As mentioned earlier, the trust and Helen's will were coordinated so that there were no conflicts, and expenses of settling her estate were minimal. Most of Helen's estate value was in trust, but there were assets which were not suited to a trust—antiques, furniture, clothing, jewelry, and so on. Helen's will disposed of some of those. What remained was sold with the proceeds deposited in her trust, which was written to make all the final dispositions.

When the will had been settled and the trust had received the will's small residue, the terms of the trust were carried out, distributing the estate to the appropriate loved ones and to the Lord's work. All of the assets of the trust not included in the will were not subject to a probate proceeding nor to the publicity a will receives. The trust in this instance was a simple and inexpensive method of distributing an estate.

Let me change the circumstances to bring out an alternate course of action which has merit. I think of an elderly widow who has taken similar action, except that she will remain as the trustee. She made her son a successor trustee so that when she becomes too weary to handle the management personally, he will assume control and manage her affairs for her. Naturally a mature relationship must exist in a case like this. The son does possess good business acumen and judgment. In this instance there can be a great degree of empathy and personal care applied to the situation. Not all families would be suited to such an agreement. Another significant factor would be that bank trustee fees would be avoided. Indeed, in both of these situations the burdens have been separated from the benefits. The trusts serve a good purpose and ultimately save a great deal of money in final settlement costs.

Let's look at a different use of the living trust which serves to separate the responsibility from the benefits. A young professional is earning resources which are accumulating beyond his living and giving habits, but form part of the provision for his long-range responsibility to his wife and perhaps other loved ones in retirement years. He has a growing practice in oral surgery and feels a tremendous need to learn, research, and gain greater personal expertise in his field. He recognizes that God is honored when he becomes a credit to his profession, and so wholeheartedly applies himself to the task of serving. The resources which are one by-product of this effort become a burden he doesn't want to carry, nor is he qualified to do so. Consequently he drops by his bank and arranges for them to take on his burden. He may begin by transferring an accumulated sum from his savings to the trust, and adding periodically to the fund.

A trust which is coordinated with his total estate planning is established. He may fund it initially with cash. The bank knows his investment objectives and seeks to carry them out. The terms are to let it grow to meet long-range needs. There will be no income distributed, and in effect it will remain rather quiet serving its one purpose of transferring management responsibility to the bank while the dentist is young.

The trust is nevertheless coordinated with his will in the event of his death. Now, unlike Helen, he has dependent minor loved ones. The trust can still serve their possible needs very well, even though he primarily establishes it for another purpose. Another thing that makes it different from Helen's trust is that only a small portion of his total estate is in the trust. The dentist has an option to add other assets to the trust any time he wishes. His will controls the disposition of fully 75 percent of his estate. Let's assume that in this instance his will contains no trust, and that all assets after his will has been settled will be placed in the living trust. So the terms of his trust will need to be clear as to how the assets are used to meet the needs of his surviving loved ones.

The dentist's wife is a good mother and a sound manager in her area of family finances. She is blessed with good judgment. The three children are growing normally—physically, mentally, and spiritually. In establishing the trust, the dentist simply leaves his wife maximum flexibility and gives her full control of all family assets, including the right to revoke or alter the trust in any way which best suits her needs. Their estate is growing, but it has not yet reached the size where it will be adversely affected by federal estate taxes. (See chapter 10.) However, it will soon be a factor and this will require some changes in planning. One of the problems in our society today is that tax laws change rapidly and our financial picture seems to constantly get out of focus. We need to be alert to make course corrections continually. I find far too many people who plan and prepare a will, then set it aside thinking it will last a lifetime.

Now the dentist and his wife both die in a car accident. Three children, all minors, survive them. The trust may continue, unhindered, serving a different purpose. The death of the parents triggers another event. All income and whatever principal there is of the assets may now be used by the guardian in cooperation with the trustee to provide for the children. The trust maintains continuity and affords more freedom. The will is administered by the executor and when the estate is settled, the remaining assets pour into the trust to provide additional financial resources for the children. Life insurance on the dentist's life, which may have initially been designated to go to his wife, had a secondary beneficiary, the trustee of the trust. There is little or no delay in collecting that and having it available too.

When will this trust terminate? Most state laws put a limit on the length of a trust. It cannot go on "in perpetuity," says the law; or in other words, for an endless period of time. You could not, for instance, specify that "this trust will continue as long as anyone who is ever related to me at any time in the future is still living." The common rule is that it may last for twenty-one years plus nine months after the life of some living person. It can serve its purpose sooner than that anyway. I find most parents are interested in helping their children through the educational process and perhaps in getting started financially for a short period beyond that. So a trust normally is designed to last until the youngest child is twenty-five or thirty years of age, in the event both parents are deceased.

Most Christian parents are keenly aware that they do not want to produce a "trust baby" out of a physically and mentally normal child. Many trust babies, adults well along in years, have become so dependent on a life-long trust income left them that they are incapable of pursuing a worthy vocation and gaining the kind of self-esteem and sense of personal worth that God intended for every individual to attain. I've met others who have not let their privileged circumstances alter their call of God to become all that he wants them to become.

What about the distribution process when the children do reach age twenty-five or thirty? Should they simply be given all of the estate regardless of its size? Not necessarily. It might be in their best interest to receive only a portion, leaving part of the final sum to be distributed to God's work. Each instance, person, and situation has to be evaluated prayerfully.

Some years ago I had the privilege of listening to a lecture on estate planning by an old professional at a well known southern university. He had devoted a lifetime to estate planning counsel. I appreciated his wisdom and candor. One day he addressed himself to the matter of what to do for your children. He said, "You know, you really only need to do two things in life for your children by way of estate planning. First, educate them in the fullest sense of the word to take their place in this world; to be professionally competent to earn their own way." My mind went back to the Word of God in Deuteronomy 6:4-7:

Hear, O Israel: The Lord our God is one Lord: and thou shalt love the Lord thy God with all thine heart, and with all thy soul, and with all thy might. And these words, which I command thee this day, shall be in thine heart: And thou shalt teach them diligently unto thy children, and shalt talk of them when thou sittest in thine house, and when thou walkest by the way, and when though liest down, and when thou risest up.

The planning we need to do for them begins early in life with attitudes, love, understanding, managing finances, and the habits of life which form the backbone for all that will follow. We need to do more than just help them become professionals; we should help them become men and women of God, equipped to be soldiers of the cross and to serve in the specific place and way God wants them to serve.

The second step we should take in estate planning for children is to so provide for ourselves as parents that we will not become dependent upon our children in later years. Admittedly, this would be ideal. All of our best-laid plans cannot always produce this result. Unforeseen illness can greatly change that objective in a short time. Then too, I think of the family unit and structure from a biblical viewpoint. Parents and children have a tremendous responsibility to one another which we all too often forget. However, I suppose, from a purely economic standpoint the old professor offered a good plan. What he said was that when the funeral was over and the expenses were paid for the survivor of the parents, ideally there would be no surplus and no debt. Economically, mother and dad would have finished as they arrived—even with the world.

Testamentary trust. The living trust is not for everyone. Some will be adequately taken care of by a testamentary trust, the type of trust created by a will.

There is a family living out west whose story will show you how this works. Jack and Peggy Wilson have three children, ages fifteen, thirteen, and ten. College years are before them and all the children look forward to attending. The Wilsons own a home, the usual personal property, a modest retirement fund, and Mr. Wilson has almost $100,000 in life insurance. The total estate including insurance would be approximately $150,000. They have a will which includes a testamentary trust. Jack's will leaves everything to Peggy, with Peggy named executrix. Peggy's will leaves everything to Jack, and Jack is nominated to be her executor. In the event both die at the same time, a suitable guardian has been named to raise the children. They share the Wilsons' Christian commitment and are admired by the Wilsons in their role as parents.

They have two children of their own.

In the event of the death of both Mr. and Mrs. Wilson, the executor is instructed to settle the estate and turn over the assets in a suitable manner to the trustee of the trust. This would probably call for selling the home and collecting the life insurance. The personal property would have to be evaluated carefully to see which items should be retained for future benefit to the children, especially those items having unique significance and sentimental value. The Wilsons need to prepare a document to be placed with their will which instructs the executor how he should distribute these items. By putting this information in a document separate from the will, the instructions can be changed easily and often. Most executors, while not bound by law to do so, will faithfully follow those instructions.

The life insurance, which in this instance is the major asset, is payable initially to Mrs. Wilson, then to the trustee of the trust contained in the Wilsons' will dated August 1972. This allows the life insurance to avoid a probate proceeding and to be immediately available to the trustee for needs which arise. When the executor, a personal friend, has completed his task, the trustee, also a personal friend, begins his duty of carrying out the terms of the Wilson trust for the benefit of the children.

You may think a trust is unnecessary in a small estate like the Wilsons'. But it gives much greater freedom to the guardian and will be far more versatile for the children. It avoids an enormous amount of red tape and problems. The children's share can be handled as in the previous illustration—spread over a greater period of time, allowing them to mature and develop a greater sense of responsibility and to grow in spiritual stature. Without the trust, the state would be bound to distribute the assets to the children at the legal age of maturity in their state. This may be eighteen or twenty-one, depending on the state.

I should qualify the warning against creating trusts which do continue for longer periods of time. These trusts could be continued because of special needs.

The first example I think of is the dependent person, regardless of age, who lacks either the physical capacity or the mental competence to assume the responsibility of property management or to earn resources sufficient to live. This person may not necessarily be in an institution but does need special consideration. He or she may simply require specialized training of a longer term to take a responsible role in society later, and therefore needs to be protected.

The second type of situation which often arises is that of an older person, most commonly a parent, who may become physically incapable or mentally incompetent, and may lack the financial resources to provide for his own needs. In either of these situations a living or testamentary trust could be established to care for a dependent loved one who has a unique circumstance accompanying his life.

A word about trustees. It is not a task to thrust on just anyone. A trustee is entitled to a fee and bears a responsibility worth considering. A close family friend would, no doubt, waive the fee. A trustee, like an executor and guardian, cannot be forced to accept the responsibility for which he has been nominated. A point to remember here is that a trust does not go wanting for lack of a trustee. Should the trustee decline, lack qualifications, or die before the trustor, an alternate, if not provided for in the trust, could be appointed. The courts will select a worthy replacement. The lack of a trustee, like the absence of an executor or guardian in a will, does not make those documents invalid. These positions may be filled later by the court.

When the trustee assumes his duty, he is required to faithfully represent the best interests of the beneficiaries according to the terms of the trust. He is required to keep accurate records and keep the beneficiaries or their representatives adequately informed. He is to manage the affairs of the trust with the same care and skill he would exert if he were managing his own property. He is to conduct his business as an ordinarily prudent man would. It is similar to the fiduciary relationship demanded of an executor. He has certain powers designated by the laws of the state in which he lives. This includes the power to hold title to property and manage, sell, exchange, apportion, repair, lease, or borrow against. He must protect it with insurance and defend it as he would his own. He usually may invest or reinvest trust assets in almost any kind of legal investment, in order to accomplish the objectives set forth in the trust document.

It is best to grant the trustee broad powers, giving him flexibility. It is more important for him to have power and authority than to be so constrained that he cannot act. And after all, if we have had sufficient confidence in him to make him trustee, then indeed trust is the essence of the agreement.

Sometimes it is best to have a cotrustee, someone who shares equally in the administration of the trust. Cotrustees often balance each other's views. However, it should be emphasized that both must act in order to exercise the power given them. Another factor here is that if one of them dies, the surviving trustee can continue exercising his power to carry out the provisions of the trust, unless the trust implicitly denies that provision.

In other instances, a successor trustee, as referred to earlier, may accomplish the same purpose with fewer problems in administration. If a cotrustee is named in order to balance the decision making process, that's important, However, if the main reason for naming a cotrustee is to provide continuity, a successor trustee might accomplish that as well with fewer administrative problems. The trust would then simply provide that the successor assume responsibility for the trust management at some given point in time or at the happening of an event. The illustration was given earlier of the elderly widow whose son would assume responsibility when she became incapacitated or died.

Serious consideration must be given to the selection of an individual as executor as opposed to the bank as executor. Each has its advantages and disadvantages. The chief consideration would probably be the size, nature, and complexity of the assets, the terms of the trust, the family relationship, the suitability of individuals being considered as trustees, the laws of the state in which the trust is drafted, and the duration planned for the trust. The job is often not easy and may well be more suitably handled by specialists.

The cost of establishing a trust, like the cost of preparing a will, is based on the time your attorney takes to complete his work. Trust management by a financial institution such as a bank usually is determined by the value of the assets entrusted to them. For instance, one bank in Colorado charges seven dollars per thousand up to $200,000, five dollars per thousand for the next $300,000, and three dollars per thousand for the next $500,000 and so on. They have a minimum fee of $500. These fees may be reduced by 25 percent if permission is granted to allow the bank to pool the funds into a common bank fund. In this instance the minimum fee is $300. For example, had the Wilsons, mentioned earlier, elected to have a bank act as trustee following this formula, their first year costs in the pooled fund would be $787.50 for the $150,000 in assets.

Tax benefits of trusts are considered in chapter 10. The many ways to give by trust and realize tax and non-tax advantages are outlined in chapter 11.

SIX
HOW TO HELP YOUR ATTORNEY

"What do you have and what do you want to do with it?" In essence that's what an attorney will ask when you go to see him about a will. Anticipate that question and you can save time and money. It's better to go to the attorney's office prepared with all of the information in hand. This information should include a written summary of the ultimate financial objective.

Here is an example of a tentative plan prepared for an attorney in a suitable format:

WILL AND TRUST INFORMATION
for
Mr. and Mrs. Howard K. Brown

Statement of purpose: It is our desire to provide for our children through their college education or its equivalent and the initial years there-after. At our death we plan to divide our final estate with our family and the work of the Lord.

FAMILY INFORMATION

Full Name _____ Howard K. Brown _____

Other names by which you are known_____ Howie _____

Address _____ 906 Temple Drive _____
_____ Denver, Colorado 80806 _____

Telephone: Home___591-1614_____Business___634-2936_____

Age___45_____ Birthplace_Evanston, Wyoming_____

Social Security Number _____ 565-24-3980 _____

Marital Status: ___Single _X_ Married ___Widowed ___Divorced ___Separated

Information on any previous marriages ___none_____

Full Name of Spouse ___Pauline L. Brown_____

Address _____ 906 Temple Drive _____
_____ Denver, Colorado 80806 _____

Telephone: Home___591-1614___ Business___none_____

Age___40_____ Birthplace ___Oshkosh, Wisconsin_____

Children and/or Other Dependents

NAME	ADDRESS	AGE
Mary Jane Brown	906 Temple Drive, Denver 80806	15
Bill Lee Brown	" " " " "	13
Wayne Kelley Brown	" " " " "	7
Ann Lynn Brown	" " " " "	3

FINANCIAL INFORMATION
Real Estate

DESCRIPTION	LOCATION	NATURE OF TITLE Such as Joint-Ownership Tenants-in-Common	DATE OF PURCHASE	COST	APPROXI- MATE VALUE
Residence	906 Temple	Joint-Ownership	1/1/70	$27,000	$52,000
Duplex	38 Derbe St.	" "	2/15/75	$42,000	$48,000

Total_$100,000

Bank or Savings Accounts

TYPE (Checking or Savings)	NAME OF INSTITUTION	APPROXIMATE BALANCE
Checking	Mountain States	$850
Savings	Thrifty Federal	$2,150
Savings	Credit Union	3,500
	Total	$6,500

Stocks, Bonds, Notes, Etc.

COMPANY	NUMBER OF SHARES	DATE OF PURCHASE	COST	APPROXIMATE VALUE
The Connecticut Fund	655	monthly	$6,550	$9,300
General Tiffany	100	6/1/70	2,000	3,800
Amalgamated Fence	50	9/30/71	500	600
Norton Feed	200	2/10/73	200	650
Idaho Electric	100	1/10/75	1,500	900
Dearborn Tractor	300	6/13/75	3,200	3,000
First Church bonds		9/10/75	1,000	2,000
			Total	$20,250

Personal Property (Automobiles, Personal Effects, Jewelry, Art, Furniture, Etc.)

DESCRIPTION	LOCATION	DATE OF PURCHASE	COST	APPROXIMATE VALUE
Ford	Residence	11/75	$6,200	$3,000
Chevrolet	"	12/76	3,800	2,400
Furniture (Inventory on file)	"			12,000
Clothing	"			2,000
Art items	"	6/75	inherited	1,500
Antique dresser	"	"	"	500
Antique chair	"	"	"	150
1976 Nomad Trailer	"	3/76	5,200	4,000
			Total	$25,550

Other Assets

Total_____

Obligations *(Notes, Mortgages, Trust Deeds, Etc.)*

DESCRIPTION	TERMS	PRESENT BALANCE
First mortgage—residence	$242 monthly	$17,800
First mortgage—duplex	$308 monthly	30,500
Credit Union—automobile	$105 monthly	950
Melody Music Co.—organ	$100 monthly	600

Total $49,850

Other Debts

DESCRIPTION	TERMS	PRESENT BALANCE
	none	

Total_____

Insurance Policies

COMPANY	TYPE OF POLICY	OWNER	BENEFICIARY	FACE VALUE	CASH VALUE
Mutual Co.	term	Mr. Brown	Mrs. Brown	$10,000	
Benefit Co.	"	"	"	5,000	
Fidelity Co.	"	"	'	50,000	

Total $65,000

Do you expect to receive an inheritance? Explain_____

Yes.   Mr. Brown $30,000   within 15 years

Yes   Mrs. Brown   10,000   within 25 years

Explain Retirement, Pension, and Profit Sharing Benefits_____

 Only retirement. Approximately $300 per month. Reduced 50%

 at Mr. Brown's death.

Annual income: Salary $ _21,500_   Spouse $_____

Investment Income: $_1,100_

Other Income: $_____   Supplementary Income Information _____

Beneficiary Information *(Person or Charitable Organization to Receive Bequest)*

NAME   ADDRESS   DESCRIPTION OF BEQUEST

 1. In the event of Howard's death everything should go to Pauline.

 2. In the event of Pauline's death everything should go to Howard.

 3. In the event Howard and Pauline die within sixty days of one another

   everything should be directed to the trust.

 4. Please have church bonds returned to church as a gift.

 5. In the event all six of us die within sixty days of one another, please divide

   the proceeds as follows:

   a. One-half to be divided equally between Howard's parents:

       Mr. and Mrs. Harry L. Brown

       1913 Wayne Drive

       Kansas City, Kansas 71602

   and Pauline's mother:

       Mrs. Victor McNeese

       87 Nike Lane

       Albuquerque, New Mexico 89301

   b. The remaining half to be divided equally between:

       1) First Church

           110 Morrison Lane

           Denver, Colorado 80803

2) American Missions, Inc.

10 Harbor Drive

Chicago, Illinois 60602

3) Interior Mission

94 York Drive

Los Angeles, California 93102

Executor: Name someone who can ably carry out the provisions of your will. Be sure to select an alternate in case your primary choice is unable to serve.

EXECUTOR	ALTERNATE
Mr. John Thomas	Mrs. Kay Sullivan
Name	Name
1123 St. Vrain Drive	164 Gladstone Street
Street Address	Street Address
Denver, Colorado 80806	Denver, Colorado 80809
City State Zip	City State Zip

Guardian: Select the person(s) you would like to assume the responsibility for raising your children. Be sure to request their permission. Here again name an alternate.

GUARDIAN	ALTERNATE
Mr. and Mrs. George Powell	Mr. and Mrs. Ted Nichols
Name	Name
912 Chestnut Street	4806 Ohio Place
Street Address	Street Address
Denver, Colorado 80806	Fort Collins, Colorado 80716
City State Zip	City State Zip

Special instructions or questions for my attorney:

1. How does our guardian work with our trustee?

2. Our alternate executor does not drive. Is this a problem?

TRUST INFORMATION:
Briefly explain what you would like this trust to accomplish for you.

- We would want this trust to function only in the event we (Mr. and Mrs. Brown) die within sixty days of one another.

- We want to provide for the normal needs our children encounter while being cared for by our guardians in addition to the expenses of their higher education.

TRUSTEE	ALTERNATE
Mr. Evan Potter	First Bank
Name	Name
1160 Devonshire Road	1 City Street
Street Address	Street Address
Denver, Colorado 80803	Denver, Colorado 80801
City State Zip	City State Zip

BENEFICIARIES OF TRUST

Mary Jane Brown	Bill Lee Brown
Name	Name
daughter 1-6-63	son 6-2-65
Relationship Date of Birth	Relationship Date of Birth
Brown residence	Brown Residence
Street Address	Street Address
City State Zip	City State Zip

Wayne Kelley Brown	Ann Lynn Brown
Name	Name
son 8-1-71	daughter 7-20-75
Relationship Date of Birth	Relationship Date of Birth
Brown residence	Brown residence
Street Address	Street Address
City State Zip	City State Zip

First Church	American Missions, Inc.
Name	Name
Relationship Date of Birth	Relationship Date of Birth
110 Morrison Lane	10 Harbor Drive
Street Address	Street Address
Denver, Colorado 80803	Chicago, Illinois 60602
City State Zip	City State Zip

Interior Missions, Inc.	
Name	Name
Relationship Date of Birth	Relationship Date of Birth
94 York Drive	
Street Address	Street Address
Los Angeles, California 93102	
City State Zip	City State Zip

TERMS OF TRUST

General instructions: ___1. Please arrange for executor to transfer proceeds from sale of assets to trustee as soon as possible.

2. In the event we both die, secondary beneficiary of insurance will be the trustee of our trust.

3. Provide for children up to age 25.

4. Limit college allowance to one-half of actual expense as an incentive to them.

5. Provide flexibility in case any child develops special needs.

6. When last child has been cared for and no more special needs exist, terminate trust with 20% going to First Church, 20% divided equally between American Missions, Inc. and Interior Missions, Inc., and the remaining 60% may be divided equally among the children.

Having defined the objective and prepared the information, it is helpful to trace your proposed course of action before going to the attorney. It becomes a sort of trial run. Should Howard die, everything goes to Pauline, and vice versa. That is simple enough. It's more complex to imagine what happens in the event Howard and Pauline both die at nearly the same time.

Upon court approval the children are assigned to the Powells as guardians. John Thomas is approved as executor and begins to carry out his duties as outlined in chapter 4. Let's assume his work is done and his final accounting to the court approved as follows (we will assume the estate has the same value as listed above)

FINAL ACCOUNTING
Estate of
Mr. and Mrs. Howard K. Brown, Deceased
Estate at date of death

Assets

Cash	$ 6,500	
Real Property	100,000	
Securities	20,250	
Personal Property	25,550	
Life Insurance	65,000	
Total Assets		$217,300

Liabilities

Mortgages	$ 48,300	
Credit Union	950	
Note	600	
Total Liabilities		-49,850

Net Worth	$167,450

Estate at Completion of Probate

Cash Received

Cash in bank	$ 6,500	
Life insurance collected	65,000	
		$ 71,500

Cash Disbursed

To liabilities	$ 49,850	
To administration and taxes	16,650	
		-66,500
Cash on hand		$ 5,000

To be Transferred to Mr. Evan Potter
Trustee, Brown Trust

Cash	$ 5,000
Personal Property	25,550
Securities (less church bonds given to church)	18,250
Real Property	100,000
Total assets on hand	$148,800

The nature of the assets transferred may differ considerably from the above. The executor in consultation with the trustee may decide to retain the mortgages on the real estate, to sell the real estate altogether, to sell the securities, or to work out some combination which, in the interest of the children, would be most beneficial to them according to the terms of the trust.

Assuming, however, that in the Brown example the above action were taken, then Mr. Potter, with court approval, assumes his responsibilities as trustee. The executor has finished his job.

The provisions of the will have been carried out, the trust now receives the assets, and Mr. Potter carries out the trust provisions. The terms the Browns stated were to provide for the normal needs the children encounter. Therefore, Mr. Potter will want to manage the trust assets in such a way as to provide the income he finds, in consultation with the guardians, the children will need. He and the Powells may decide to keep withdrawals from the trust as low as possible for the next three years in order to let the assets grow more rapidly in anticipation of Mary's college needs, which will arise in three years. The immediate needs can vary greatly in view of special medical or dental requirements, choice of colleges, and so on. Mr. Potter's responsibility will span twenty-two years until Ann, now age three, is twenty-five. This is a gigantic task, one which should cause parents to weigh carefully their choice of a trustee, especially the decision to appoint an individual rather than a corporate trustee.

Now let's assume twenty-two years have passed, and Ann is twenty-five. According to the terms of the trust, the Browns want the remaining trust assets distributed as follows:

20% to First Church
10% to American Missions, Inc.

10% to Interior Missions, Inc.
60% divided equally among the four children

In many instances older children receive percentage distributions as they each attain twenty-five rather than waiting until the youngest reaches twenty-five. However, in this example no distributions were made until Ann was twenty-five. With all the economic uncertainties of a twenty-two-year period of time, we'll say Mr. Potter has $40,000 left in the trust fund. It is allocated as follows:

$ 8,000 to the First Church
   4,000 to American Missions, Inc.
   4,000 to Interior Missions, Inc.
  24,000 to the children ($6,000 to each of the four)
$40,000

Now let's look at it graphically to follow the flow of action:

From Brown estate $167,450

To Executor
$167,450

Church gift	-2,000
Administration and taxes	-16,650
	$148,800

To Trustee
$148,800

For family care of children	-108,800
Remainder	$ 40,000

To Final Beneficiaries

First Church	$ 8,000
American Missions, Inc.	4,000
Interior Missions, Inc.	4,000
Children	24,000
	$ 40,000

Charting the course of action is the only sure way of knowing where the resources you possess are headed.

Recently I called our bank to make a teletransfer of funds from our savings account to our checking account. In proper fashion I followed the instructions on my little wallet-size card. "I would like to transfer $500 from savings account #1-302164 to checking account #049501." The voice on the other end said, "May I have the last four digits of your Social Security number, please?" I responded, "4982." "All right," she said, "today we will transfer $500 from savings account #1-302164 to checking account #049501." I thanked her and the conversation was ended. The communication was clear and correct because I knew what I wanted done and I knew she knew what I wanted done.

Too often in will and trust preparation a family may have in mind a general idea of their intentions and arrive at their attorney's office with the ideas vaguely formulated. The attorney will listen, record key items of information, and promise to prepare their documents as instructed. Because the clients were vague, the attorney must fill in his interpretation of what he thinks they wish done. The final work may or may not match the clients' real intentions. The attorney is uncertain because the clients were uncertain.

All too often when the attorney calls and schedules fifteen minutes for the signing of the wills, the clients are given copies and asked to read them and ask any questions. Frequently, all of this is done in haste with the thought that "we will sign now and read it later." Another thing that happens is that a person may think he understands when he does not. Many attorneys wisely mail preliminary drafts of wills to their clients to let them read, think about, and question the provisions. When and only when they understand do the draftsmen proceed to prepare the instruments for the signatures.

To avoid miscommunications:

1) Prepare your information and intentions in writing ahead of time.

2) Request preliminary documents to study and be sure you understand the terminology.

3) Then trace the flow of action as we did with the Browns to be sure the result is as you intended.

A complete set of information forms are in the appendix for you to fill in and take to your attorney in order that he may prepare your will. When you help your attorney in this manner, he will be very grateful, and so will your loved ones.

SEVEN
TRAIN YOUR WIFE
TO BE A WIDOW

I stepped out of my front door and looked up and down the street. The thought occurred to me that any of the wives who live on our street could be widows by tomorrow. In fact, one Wednesday during the summer I was mowing my lawn, and as I neared my neighbor's boundary I saw him standing close by. I turned off the mower and we talked for ten or fifteen minutes. We discussed the trees, the lawn, the weather, and matters of mutual neighborhood interest. Two days later he was gone and his wife was a widow. I wondered if she were ready. Is anyone completely ready? Had he trained his wife to be a widow?

Shirley and Sam live up the street. I know them well. I decided to ask Sam if Shirley were prepared for the possibility of widowhood. Sam replied, "I don't think so. I suppose we don't really want to think about it yet. What's involved?" Sam and Shirley have been married three years and have a little girl, Sally, a year old. They own their home and one car. Sam is twenty-nine, an account executive with a large utility company. Shirley is a skilled office worker-turned-mother. She is twenty-seven.

In answer to Sam's question, "What's involved?" I

began with the first and probably most important question, "Do you and Shirley have a will?"

"No," answered Sam, "but we've been thinking about it, especially since Sally arrived on the scene."

"It's time for action," I replied and went over the essentials as outlined in chapter 3 regarding a will. To motivate him, I talked to Sam about the hardships Shirley could encounter should he die without a will (items covered in chapter 2). Next we discussed advisors.

"Who is your attorney, Sam?"

"We don't have one," he answered. "Never had a need."

"Now is the time," I replied. We considered several possibilities. In this context I suggested he think about at least two financial advisors who might be available to help Shirley in her initial decision making responsibilities.

I asked, "Sam, who writes the checks in your house?"

"I do," he said.

"Why don't you let Shirley do it two or three months of the year and also let her reconcile the bank account so that she becomes familiar with the procedure?"

"Not a bad idea," Sam acknowledged.

I continued, "She needs to know where bank statements are and cancelled checks, savings passbooks, and so on. She should know account numbers, the location of information, officers or officials you work with, and telephone numbers," I added.

Then we talked about insurance. I decided to ask Shirley a few questions. "Shirley, how much life insurance does Sam have?"

"Oh, I'm not sure. I think it's through his company though."

"Who is your automobile insurance with, Shirley?"

"Charlie, our friend, wrote the policy, but I don't remember the company name. I would just call Charlie if I needed help."

"How about homeowner's insurance?" I inquired.

"Oh, that's Charlie too . . . I think!"

"One more insurance question, Shirley. Who handles your health plan?"

"That I'm sure of because of my stay in the hospital last year."

"Sam," I said, "you need to make her a list—companies, coverage, policy numbers, amounts, and agents' names, addresses, and phone numbers."

Sam outlined for me more of his financial affairs and investments. We talked about the documents Shirley should know about—the deed to the home, title, insurance policy, and the household inventory. I suggested that Sam go through their home and make a detailed inventory of household goods, room by room, together with estimated costs, identification numbers where applicable, and today's values. I even suggested he take a picture of each room and then put the file with this information in his safe deposit box or in an appropriate file at work. "By the way, Sam," I added, "I would suggest that both of you empty the contents of your wallets and inventory them too—credit card numbers and any other documents you carry." One method I use is to simply place the items from my wallet on a photocopying machine and photocopy the contents periodically.

"Be sure Shirley knows where you keep automobile registration information, income tax returns, keys, military records, V.A. information, and marriage and birth certificates." I told them about a widow I was helping recently who could not find her marriage certificate. We contacted the county records office in the county where she and her husband were married, told them the date, and within a week she received the document which the Social Security Administration required in order to start her benefits.

"Now let's talk about your home. Does Shirley know where to find the financial data regarding the cost, improvements, escrow closing details, date of purchase?" Shirley seemed to know some of the information and be in doubt about some. Sam filled in missing information as we discussed it.

"Now here is a subject I really don't like to bring up," I continued, ". . . debts. Sam, you will want to be sure Shirley knows about any debts you may have, the terms for payments, amounts, to whom, when, and the location of documents."

I suggested to Sam that a major item of importance to convey to Shirley was some idea of his desires about a funeral and any special form of service he would like. Thinking this through ahead of time and coming to some conclusions would spare her the tough decisions at a time when decisions would be difficult to make.

Having stirred Sam and Shirley's minds quite enough for one day, I departed to let them think and plan. Sometime later Sam prepared a "Memo to My Wife" document which looked something like this:

Memo to My Wife

OUR WILL

Our will is located ___in safe deposit box 6319, First National Bank___

The executor who is designated to carry out the provisions of our will is ___Jerry Beam___

If___Jerry___decline(s) or cannot serve, the alternate is ___Bill Sloane___

Our attorney is___Jon Edmund___ (phone: ___633-1020___)
and should be consulted to assist you in settling any of the legal matters you need help with.

In the event our estate is subject to estate tax, our accountant is___Don Roscoe___
(phone:___634-9801___). Two other people (financial advisors) I recommend to assist you with financial matters are___Jim Deeson___phone: ___634-7811___
and___Gary Ripple___ phone:___633-1140___

The main provisions of the will are: ___I leave everything to you when I die.___
___You leave everything to me when you die. In the event we both___
___die at nearly the same time, everything goes in trust for Sally.___

TRUST

Our will includes a trust. The main provisions of the trust are:

Trustee: __Bill Sloane__ Alternate: First National Bank

Assets in the trust: __equity from home sale, insurance proceeds, company benefits, investments, personal property__

Beneficiaries: __Sally and First Church__

Terms: __Support Sally through college. One-half to Sally at age 25, one-fourth to Sally at age 30, and remainder to the First Church.__

BANKING

Our checking account is familiar to you. However, I talked with __George Redman__, our banker at the __First National__ Bank (phone: __634-1067__) who told me the following information which relates to our account in the event of my death: __You may have immediate access to $5,000. In about two weeks the remainder will be released.__

Our account number(s) are __1-490-480__

Information about other checking accounts and location of checkbooks: __lower left storage in bedroom closet__

Our bank statements and canceled checks may be found __basement storage—file drawer #4__

Similar information pertaining to our savings account(s) is as follows:

1 Account number: __1-694-039__
   Name of Savings Institution: __Valley Federal Savings__
2 Account number: __394-689__
   Name of Savings Institution: __First National Bank__
3 Account number: _____
   Name of Savings Institution: _____

Our passbooks are located __green file box in bedroom__

Special information relating to these accounts in the event of my death: __These are in joint ownership with rights of survivor, which means the ownership passes to you after a brief waiting period.__

INSURANCE

At the end of this booklet is a list of the life insurance policies on my life. You will want to collect these proceeds as soon as possible to help with the expenses.

Call our agent Paul Gilliom (phone: 637-9072) to help you or have your financial advisor or attorney help you with this. You may write the companies directly, enclosing a copy of the death certificate.

Also included is a list of the life insurance policies on your life and the children's lives for your information. The policies on all of our lives are located:

In the lower right compartment of the desk

The homeowners policy is with American Security Company

That policy (# 1A-642-393-1) is located desk—lower right compartment

The automobile insurance is with American Security (phone: 695-1806)

The policy is located desk—lower right compartment

Our medical insurance is with Fidelity Medical Company (Phone: 634-5992)

The policy number is 16-49-3982 and is located desk—lower right compartment

INVESTMENTS

Our stock broker Jim Nelson with Harley-Wallace Company

(address: Union Grove Building and phone: 633-9876) has given me a complete list of our stocks and bonds as of 12/31/79 which is attached. As you know, this list and values often change. Notify him of my passing so that he can change his records.

Title to the stocks and bonds is as follows: Mr. and Mrs. with rights of survivor. The transfer is handled similarly to other assets, in that the death certificate is required to produce proof of my death for transfer of ownership.

The actual certificates are located In Jim Nelson's office.

DOCUMENTS

The deed to our home is located _in the safe deposit box_

and it reads that we own it (nature of title) as _joint tenants with rights_

of survivor.

I feel the value is approximately $ _45,000_ The mortgage balance is $30,000.

The files which pertain to the home such as cost of purchase, improvements, original

closing, etc. are marked _1. 905 Tulip Street, 2. Home improvements_

and are located _in file drawer #4 in the basement_

I made an inventory of our household furnishings together with the approximate

values. That inventory is located _in the safe deposit box_

The attached photocopy shows the contents of my wallet. If I am killed in an accident and the wallet is not recovered, you will want to notify the credit card companies that the cards have been lost.

Just a reminder about our safe deposit box(es):

No. _6398_ No.: _____

Located _in the First National Bank_

The key(s) is/are _in lower right desk compartment_

All the birth certificates are located _in the safe deposit box_

Other important documents and their locations are as follows:

Automobile titles/registrations _safe deposit box_

Income tax returns _file drawer #2—basement_

Keys _extra keys in center desk drawer_

Military records _file drawer #2—basement_

Naturalization/citizenship papers _— —_

Patents and copyrights _— —_

Title insurance _in the safe deposit box_

Marriage Certificate _safe deposit box_

Veterans Administration information _file drawer #2—basement_

MY MILITARY HISTORY:

Service Number   568-21-60

Branch of Service U.S. Navy

Length of Service 3 years

From 12/70 to 12/73

Rank   Petty Officer 2nd Class

Location of special papers:

Document	Location
D.D. #214	file drawer #2—basement

Contents of Safe Deposit Box: 1. Our wills

2. Deed to our home

3. Household inventory

4. Photocopy of our wallet contents

5. Auto titles

6. Birth and marriage certificates

7. Title insurance

Other real estate we own is as follows:

Description	Location
1. frame house	905 Tulip Street
2.	Colorado Springs, Colorado
3.	
4.	

The file where more information
is kept about this property is located   safe deposit and file drawer #2 basement

Nature of Title Such as Joint-Ownership Tenants-in-Common	Mortgage Balance	Date of Purchase	Cost	Value
1. joint ownership	$30,000	8/75	$42,000	$45,000
2.				
3.				
4.				

Total $45,000

The deeds are located   safe deposit and file drawer #2 basement

DEBTS WE OWE

Here is an explanation of some long-term obligations which are not a normal part of our monthly budget:

Description	Terms	Present Balance	Location of Document
Auto	3-year	$3,200	safe deposit box

LIST OF INSURANCE POLICIES   Date_____

(Husband) Name and Address of Company and Local Agent	Policy Number	Face Value	Loan Balance Which Will be Deducted	Approximate Net Amount Due You
1. Equitable Assurance	#649-310-19	$45,000	none	$45,000
2.				
3.				
4.				
5.				

LIST OF INSURANCE POLICIES   Date_____

(Wife and children) Name and Address of Company and Local Agent	Policy Number	Face Value	Loan Balance Which Will be Deducted	Approximate Net Amount Due You
1. _____(Shirley)_____	#619304-A	$15,000	---	$15,000
2. _____(Sally)_____	#1639413	$2,000	----	$2,000
3.				
4.				
5.				

FUNERAL INSTRUCTIONS

Funeral Home_____ Anderson Funeral Home _____

Address _____ 619 N. Curley _____

Phone_____ 634-9821 _____

☒ 1 I direct that my body be used for medical purposes as follows: _____ organ
transplants as needed _____

☒ 2 I request post-mortem examination be made if desirable.

☐ 3 I direct cremation of remains.

    ☐ No ashes to remain

    ☐ Disposition of ashes as follows:

_____

_____

_____

☒ 4 I request burial in the following manner:
_____cemetery plot_____

_____

_____

_____

Place of burial:_____Greenlawn Cemetery_____
Address ____605 W. Tilson_____

☐ 5 I wish memorial service with no casket present.

☒ 6 I desire a funeral with remains present:

    ☒ Closed casket   ☐ Open casket

    (Special information: _open casket for immediate family, if desired_____

_____

☒ 7 Service:

    a. Church__First Church_____

    b. Clergyman _____senior pastor_____

    c. Prelude _____"Be Still, My Soul"_____

    d. Solo _____George White_____

    e. Hymns_____"In the Garden"_____

    f. Special Scripture or poems_____
_____1 Corinthians 15_____

    g. Other instructions _____

_____

_____

_____

_____

☐ 8 I request that memorial gifts be given to the following:
Church or organization____First Church_____
Address ____619 W. Rio Grande_____
Other information:

_____

Signed _____Sam Smith_____
Witnesses:

_____ Date_____
_____ Date_____
_____ Date_____

At Sam's request I reviewed the entire contents and was deeply impressed with his good work. "Now," I said, "when would you like to know the rest?"

"The rest!" he exclaimed. "How could there be more?"

"Sit down, Sam. Let's talk," I began. "There is another area we should discuss. It's what I call 'maintenance management' and I have this information in a handy file folder where Patty has ready access to it—not only in preparation for the possibility of my death but for her use during my travels. Here is the way it reads:

HOUSEHOLD

Electrical (all repairs & appliances)	Appliance Service Company 312 North Winter 399-3136
Main switch	Top switch, gray box over first shelf in garage.
Plumbing/heating	Right Plumbing & Heating 3120 West Utah 398-6127
Water	Shut off valve with red tag on it marked "shut off" near hot water heater.
Gas	Shut off east side of house.

YARD

Lawn and garden	Dave's Nursery 1130 West Unfeld 399-5244

Some wives are mechanically inclined and know the whereabouts of tools, how to plunge the toilets, repair blown fuses, fix the fence, and so on. Others need the above information and more to help them in the absence of their husbands.

It was just past noon one fine fall day. Our elders' meeting was ten minutes under way when our minister's secretary popped through the door to let me know that Patty was on the phone. "Honey," she said frantically, "I just came home for lunch and the laundry room toilet is running over into the room and into the basement from all directions. Where does the water turn off?" Fine husband I am! She didn't know because I hadn't told her, and in the confusion of the moment I failed to tell her she could have reached below the toilet and shut off the water at the valve. I said, "Hold on, here I come" . . . and five minutes later it was under control. We have been married only twenty-six years. I just hadn't gotten around to letting her know a few of my secrets!

There is a common line of thought that about January 1 we ought to stop, review our lives, take an inventory of sorts, and rededicate ourselves to a new set of priorities and objectives. It is a kind of fresh-start thing with us. Why not set aside a day between Christmas and New Year's to stop and evaluate all the things your wife should know if she should become a widow on January 1?

Start with a review and update of "Memo to My Wife." Is it current? Reread the wills and trusts. You will be amazed at how quickly they become outdated. Chapter 8 will provide a context for a discussion on finances. That may be the most important part. Wives whose husbands are always home and never travel have the biggest adjustment to make, because they have a hard time imagining how to live without them.

Sit down and imagine that he is gone and how you would handle the home, the yard, the automobiles, the finances, investments, life insurance, funeral, and so on. Ask the questions now. It is startling how little husbands tell their wives about their part of the family management affairs. Talk to some widows and you will discover frustration along these lines to the extent of bitterness. So many widows simply say, "Oh, he didn't want to bother me with financial matters!" Alone, without a basis for decisions along these lines, she is at the mercy of all kinds of poor advisors; and unless she is almost aggressive in pursuing this, she will suffer more than many of us realize. Given basic information and some guidelines for financial discussion, women will equal or surpass men in financial management. This may possibly be why some husbands do not inform their wives. There may be a subtle fear that the wife will take away a cherished role all red-blooded American males desire. But good leadership means we train our replacements and train them well. So goes the scriptural leader-father in the home. If he is capable, he will be sure she can assume all his part of the family management role in his absence. This will contribute substantially to her peace of mind and to the benefit of their children, who will have a serious enough loss to adjust to.

EIGHT
THE WIDOW'S BUDGET

Recently an insurance company reported that 52 percent of all U. S. widows had spent all their husbands' death benefits within eighteen months. They added that the average U. S. widow receives only $12,000 in benefits including all insurance, Social Security, pensions, and veterans benefits. It seems apparent that the vast majority of widows simply do not have adequate financial resources to meet their needs. I wondered why. What are the reasons husbands leave their wives without resources?

They refuse to consider the possibility that they could die prematurely. This is probably the major reason people don't have wills. They irrationally feel that if they write a will, death is on their doorstep. This is neither thoughtful nor realistic.

They think Social Security will pay all the bills. It is amazing to me how much people think Social Security will do for them. It is a marvelous system but certainly is not intended to provide complete financial support. The gap between the time the youngest child turns eighteen and the widow reaches sixty can be long and is entirely without help from Social Security. Social Security's greatest strength is helping out while children are under eighteen. Often when the widow becomes sixty, the benefits are "slim pickin's"; and if she begins to draw upon those benefits at sixty, she must take a lower benefit than she would receive at sixty-five.

Let me share one woman's budget with you. Freda is sixty-two and has moderate health problems. Several of us help her in a variety of ways. My job is to help her keep her bank account in order. She lives alone in a studio apartment on the east side of town. Her Social Security benefit is $209 and her company retirement benefit $86—a total of $295. Her housing alone is $137.50 a month, low by many standards, but too high in proportion to her income—46 percent. All housing costs, including utilities, should not exceed 30 percent. One of our concerns is to find adequate housing priced in proportion to her income. By the guideline of 30 percent, her entire housing costs could not exceed $88.50. That is not realistic, but that *is* her problem. Imagine if Social Security was all Freda had—she would be dependent on others. Another way to look at it is to suppose she had *no* Social Security! She and thousands of others would be totally dependent on loved ones.

They think their wives will marry again soon. It is not realistic to believe that our widows will immediately or even eventually remarry. Many are attractive and youthful, but may be surrounded by two or more lively children, who are not so attractive to a prospective husband. Many a prospective new husband withdraws when he sees a houseful of children, who are sometimes downright belligerent at the possibility of some strange man coming on the scene as a stepfather.

Even given the right man, a widow often has a traumatic recovery from the loss of her husband which may take years. The adjustments are more than we can imagine. Marriage is simply not imminent, and the very worst thing we can do is to plan that way in our minds, perhaps forcing our widows into making a hasty marital choice due to their impending economic crisis.

They would rather earmark all their resources for future retirement. 1 Timothy 5:8 reads in *The Living Bible,* "But anyone who won't care for his own relatives when they need help, especially those living in his own family, has no right to say he is a Christian. Such a person is worse than the heathen." I think this verse not only means providing for what a family needs now, but also making provision for them for after our death. Too many fail to plan for this and drift day by day toward retirement without consideration of loved ones. Death is unwanted, even with all of Paul's anticipation, the scriptural admonition to be ready, and the joy of meeting Jesus face to face. I don't think most of us wake up saying to ourselves that maybe today will be the day I will slip into glory! And that's only human, for we have families, responsibilities, and people here we don't want to leave. Not wanting to leave, we refuse to plan for what we would consider our premature departure. Since retirement is a more favorable alternative, we plan for that. But when you know that 75 percent of today's wives become widows, you realize some thought and planning must go into this part of a husband's responsibility to provide for loved ones.

They have not stopped to consider the financial consequences of their death. Ask a husband sometime if he has actually stopped to add up the dollar-and-cents results of his possible death. Sometimes we read statistics of how many people do not have wills. This ranges from 60 percent to 80 percent, depending on what you read. I have found that the thoughtful husband who has a will often tucks it away with a false sense of security that he has done it all—no more thought need be given to his potential death or its consequences. Additionally, it is amazing how few pull out those old wills and reread them to discover that they have become inadequate or even null and void by the passing of time or by some event.

Let's consider the financial consequences for a Colorado Springs family I know. Jack and Betty are forty-seven and forty-two respectively, with three children, two in college and one at home. They begin by going over the family budget to determine what Betty's needs would be should Jack die soon. Here are their conclusions:

Monthly Budget for Betty

Mortgage or Rental (Insurance/Taxes too)	$ 325.00
Utilities	75.00
Household/Yard/Furnishings	60.00
Food/Household	200.00
Auto Expense (including insurance/repair/license)	80.00
Clothing & Personal Care	80.00
Education	200.00
Charitable Contributions	125.00
Gifts & Allowances	75.00
Medical & Dental	75.00
Vacation & Recreation	75.00
Life Insurance	10.00
Miscellaneous	25.00
Other	
Car Replacement	100.00
Taxes	150.00
Total Expense	$1,655.00

Now they consider the resources available to meet those needs. They own their own home, which has a value of $65,000 and a loan of $30,000. Jack has $92,000 in life insurance and an additional $50,000 in accidental death benefits. We rule out the accidental death benefit, because at Jack's age less than 10 percent of deaths occur as the result of an accident. Jack has $3,000 in stock but no other assets. Small debts also amount to about $3,000. All personal property is paid for. Jack and Betty summarize her potential income as a widow as follows:

Company benefit	$	75
Investment income*		567
Betty's salary		750
Total income		$1,392

*Life insurance	$92,000
Less final expenses	7,000
	$85,000 invested at 8% = $6,800

$6,800 ÷ 12 months = $567

So Betty's monthly income would be $263 below her budget. By looking at the prospective financial consideration now, Jack can help Betty decide how to solve some problems and do some planning. They have three choices: 1) raise the income, 2) reduce the expenses, or 3) do both.

We begin by examining the expenses. We could eliminate the house payments by paying off the mortgage. The question now is whether Betty will want to stay where she is for a number of years. They discuss that choice and decide yes, Betty would be comforted by remaining in the family home for an indefinite period of time. If it is not clear how the mortgage should be handled, it would be best for Jack and Betty to leave the mortgage alone until the Lord leads in some definite way.

Frequently widows automatically pay off the mortgage. They are far more uneasy about debt with their husbands gone. However, should there be some possibility that she would sell the family home in the near future, the mortgage may actually increase the value of the home. A mortgage with a low interest rate, which may be assumed by a prospective buyer, keeps the payment down and interest costs lower. A mortgage like that, if it has a fairly high balance due in relation to the home value, is especially helpful in a sale.

But what would be the financial consequences of removing the mortgage?

Analysis of Widow's Income

Tentative budget		$1,655
Less mortgage		-325
		$1,330
Add taxes	$65	
Add insurance	15	+80
	New budget	$1,410
Tentative income		$1,392
Less: $30,000 used to pay mortgage		
(30,000 x 8% ÷ 12)		-200
	New income	$1,192

	With Mortgage	Without Mortgage
Estimated budget	$1,655	$1,410
Available resources	-1,392	-1,192
Deficit	$ 263	$ 218

In effect, by removing the mortgage we have reduced Betty's need by a net $45 monthly. Let's assume that will be Jack's recommendation to Betty. We still have to solve a $218 deficit.

A reanalysis of expenses causes Jack and Betty to evaluate some important items. The easy way out would be to cut out the $200 allocation for education. Each child will receive Social Security until age eighteen or twenty-two if enrolled in college. Let them work for the remaining tuition and living expenses.

By eliminating that item and $18 from one or more other areas, the immediate needs could be met without difficulty.

We are right back to a rather basic issue: what is God's will for Jack and Betty? The financial planners of our time would probably not take this simple and obvious approach. Most planners feel you should plan an income for your widow's entire life and exclude the possibility of her earning an income. Therefore, how much would Betty need for a lifetime income if she became a widow now? Inflation must be considered, fluctuating interest rates, and life expectancy. If Betty lives to age seventy-seven, she will live thirty-five years. Let's trim her budget to, say, an average of $12,000 a year. Let's also assume her cash invested could earn 8 percent a year in earnings, but be decreased by 5 percent inflation. Her funds would then increase a net 3 percent. Betty would need $265,584 at the time of Jack's death. If she put this in an investment, let it earn 8 percent a year which would be estimated to lose 5 percent a year to inflation, Betty could withdraw $12,000 a year and it would last until she was seventy-seven years old. The $265,584 would be offset by her right to receive certain Social Security funds in the future, her current assets at Jack's death, and the present value of her projected earnings should she elect to earn a salary. These are the criteria many planners use to calculate the financial needs a widow may have.

But, I think this approach puts the emphasis on the wrong subject—money. The emphasis, it seems to me, should be on the person. For years in America we have emphasized family endowments—that is, funds for lifetime support of family members. What these produce is people who simply depend on their money which month by month flows into their lives. In many instances the results have been disastrous.

When we supply someone with a lifetime income, we deprive them of a unique opportunity to develop as a person. Their need to walk by faith is eroded, as is their need to learn and grow and trust God. Jack's and Betty's plan for her to continue working would seem far better than total provision by Jack's estate.

Jack and Betty are beginning to plan. It is a healthy start. It is miles ahead of most people who have failed to at least look at the future and consider what will happen. Jack is not in a position to fund the whole future for Betty. The really important step they have taken is to plan the eventuality together and give Betty a start into a world of thinking which is unfamiliar to her. This is putting the emphasis on Betty. This is equipping her to walk her remaining years, if God so leads, unmarried.

If this is logical thinking, and I think it is, then let's focus on Betty for a moment. Right now she would say, in view of Jack's being alive, that her calling is primarily to be a wife and mother. If Jack dies, a large part of her life is gone. Being a mother is still important, but soon their one remaining child will be out of the nest and gone. Betty will be alone—or will she?

What next? Where is she needed? Suppose Jack and Betty think and plan along those lines now. Betty is a beautiful person in more ways than one. She is a vital part of the body of Christ, but as in the case of many wives she is perhaps overshadowed by her husband's endeavors—a tribute to her humility. Exit Jack, and we have a different picture. Why not begin now to help and train Betty in areas in which she is gifted to become all that God has in mind for her to become? Why not enable her now, with only one child at home, to become equipped to play a more meaningful and significant role in the work of Christ? We are talking about career planning for Betty.

Guess what widows suffer from the most, even more

than lack of finances. Loneliness. Why? Because the central concern of their lives (apart from the Lord) is gone.

Maybe the real investment should begin with Betty. There is a balance. Betty could be a professional nurse, teacher, accountant, or secretary with a sound future economically, and a promising opportunity for serving within the body of Christ. This would not free her from need of financial resources in the event of Jack's death. This does not eliminate the need for Betty and Jack to plan together and for her to be fully informed in areas unfamiliar to her. Every wife, regardless of her background and training, needs to say to her husband, "How much money do I need and what do I need to know if you die tomorrow?"

Now let's look at another active couple I was involved with some months ago in California. Susana was born in 1896 and Floyd in 1890. Some people feel age is a deterrent to being a meaningful, significant person, that sixty-five is the end—time for the rocking chair, TV, soap operas, crossword puzzles, and tours. Not Susana. At age eighty-one, when she became a widow, she became more active. Why should she stop now? I've watched her. Let me share her financial circumstances. Her husband left her a small comfortable home, no mortgage, enough investments to earn about $200 a month, no company benefits, no life insurance. His body was a gift to medical research so the total mortuary cost was $75. Susana's Social Security income is $312 a month. To summarize:

Income:

Social security	$312
Investment income	200
Total income	$512

She is well able to live within her income. However, she is a creative person and very gifted in art, particularly children's art. After Floyd's death she continued hard at work teaching, painting, and pursuing her writing with more fervor, anxious to reach some important personal objectives. The last time I checked on her whereabouts and her welfare she was on the go, lecturing in New York, Connecticut, and Vermont. Within two weeks she would be on her way to South America for a month. Life has meaning and significance to Susana. Oh, there was an adjustment and loneliness to be sure, but Floyd had encouraged and helped her to become the fully developed person she as an individual was meant to become. Who knows how long she will be making her contribution felt? That's exciting to me.

Too many widows are sitting back, mad at Social Security for not feeding them, bitter at their husbands for not providing for them, and seething in self-pity and loneliness.

Some years ago I remember meeting with a West Coast widow in her sixties who, in discussing her future, remarked about her destiny, "You see, John, I was born to be somebody." She had a positive outlook, a significance that was vital to her life and performance and sense of well-being. If only we could each, widows included, see how significant we are to God, we would be more highly motivated to get the most out of life and to give the most to it.

The emphasis then focuses on the person and the effect of death on her life and calling. Rather than withdrawing, she should see opportunity ahead. Paul said, "For because of our faith, he has brought us into this place of highest privilege where we now stand, and we confidently and joyfully look forward to actually becoming all that God has had in mind for us to be (Romans 5:2, *The Living Bible*).

There is nothing more vital to us in the arena of life than to be convinced of the sovereignty of God, to believe in our hearts that God is in control and that we have a purpose and significance to him. What a priceless resource this becomes! It is, of course, also economically sound to be a well-equipped person.

Having prepared a budget, having examined the available resources, what course of action should Jack and Betty pursue? Cut expenses, secure more resources? How much will be enough in terms of more resources? Where will the resources end and faith for the future begin as they so intertwine as to become inseparable? Jack and Betty will now give serious thought to Betty's future, her career. She has had two years of college in education. Should she return to school and obtain a teaching credential? At forty-two has she lost too much of her educational intake to pick it up again? Is teaching a field with a promising future? Should she continue now in the financial field, where she is serving, and perhaps pursue further skills there? There are lots of questions, important questions for Jack and Betty and many other couples who need to consider the financial circumstances of one future event, death, which may occur at any time.

NINE
BEFORE YOU
BUY INSURANCE

The two most important future economic events you face are retirement and death. While retirement needs our attention, only the financial consequences of death will be considered here.

Insurance nearly always forms a vital part of the estate of the family breadwinner. Before you buy life insurance you should know the answers to four key questions:

1. What is the purpose intended?
2. How much insurance is enough?
3. What type of insurance will do the job?
4. What company offers me the best value?

Let's begin with a brief overview of life insurance. In essence life insurance is money—money to replace money lost by someone's death. It is protection. Pure insurance is pure protection. David Martin is thirty and asks his insurance company to insure him for $10,000 until he is sixty-five. He pays $73.50 every year. If he dies, his widow receives $10,000 (the face value of the policy). She is "protected" against a portion of the economic loss she would incur by the death of her husband. In a sense it is like a fire insurance policy on a home. David may determine that it would take $45,000 to replace his home should a fire destroy it. He buys a fire insurance policy which, in the event fire destroys his home, will pay him $45,000. This is pure protection.

The life insurance industry refers to pure protection insurance as *term insurance*, as it provides an economic benefit to the insured's beneficiaries for a given "term" of years. Sometimes people insure themselves until age sixty-five, seventy, or even to a hundred. There are different ways to buy term insurance. They are discussed later in this chapter.

If you would like to buy more than protection in your life insurance policy, you may establish a savings account with your insurance company. You now have protection and savings, or what is called *cash value insurance*. All insurance falls into these two categories, term and term with cash value. David Martin, age thirty, decides to insure his life for $10,000 (face value), but also wants to have the insurance company establish a savings element in the policy. He pays an annual premium of $142.50. Each year his savings account grows, but in essence his protection decreases. Look at it this way.

	Term		Term with Cash Value	Age 65
$10,000		$10,000		
			Protection	$ 4,500
	Protection			
			Cash Value	5,500
Age 30		65 Age 30	65	$10,000

To summarize then, all life insurance is protection or protection plus savings.

What is the purpose intended? Buyers of life insurance have one of three purposes.

Some use the savings in life insurance as an *invest-*

ment avenue to meet some short or long-term objective ranging from costs of a college education in twenty years to a supplement for retirement needs at age sixty-five. Volumes are written on the relative suitability of insurance as an investment. It is not within the scope of this study to evaluate insurance as an investment. However, if a person's insurance premiums are high and the face value of the policy is low as a result of unusually high "investments" in cash value insurance, this may seriously affect the survivors in a family who have lost the major source of their income through death. This is a vital factor in the welfare of the loved ones we leave behind, because the principal purpose for life insurance is *protection*.

For example, a family whose chief provider is thirty years old may feel they can afford only $25 a month for life insurance. This would probably produce less than $15,000 in coverage on his life in a typical whole life policy paid up at age sixty-five; whereas he could obtain from $60,000 to $75,000 worth of protection should he choose a term policy. Evaluate the reduction in death benefits as a result of an unusual purchase of cash value insurance. This is of critical importance in planning.

Two objectives need to be considered: 1) a future need we save to meet—for example, college or retirement, and 2) death benefits for our survivors' needs. These objectives must be viewed separately and planned with a balanced sense of responsibility. Thus, investment as well as protection has become a purpose for obtaining life insurance.

Still a third purpose for obtaining life insurance may combine both protection and investment elements. It is what is called *estate liquidity*. Joe and Diane Ross own a ranch in eastern New Mexico. They are in their early fifties and have acquired sizable holdings in both farmland and grazing land. The value of their estate is over $1,000,000 and growing. One day it occurred to Joe that if he died, Diane would need to come up with nearly $150,000 in cash within nine months to meet tax and administrative expenses because of the value of their estate. Examining the nature of their estate, he realized Diane would be virtually without any ready cash to meet those needs. So they began an aggressive savings program to begin to put them in a more flexible position. In addition, they planned certain other types of investments for the future, giving them more flexibility and cash. To supplement their changed investment strategy they also purchased decreasing-term life insurance policies on both of their lives to cover the intervening years while they reapportioned their assets. Joe and Diane's estate might look like this:

	1978	1983	1988
Land & buildings	$ 800,000	$ 950,000	$1,100,000
Equipment	75,000	85,000	95,000
Cattle	100,000	110,000	120,000
Personal property	15,000	17,000	20,000
Cash & savings	5,000	6,000	7,000
*Insurance - Joe	100,000	75,000	50,000
*Insurance - Diane	100,000	75,000	50,000
Liquid investments (income earning)	---	25,000	50,000
Totals	$1,195,000	$1,343,000	$1,492,000

*Purchased after the need for tax funds was discovered.

Now if Joe dies, Diane has ready access to at least $100,000. The same applies to Joe if Diane dies. But as the years pass, the insurance needs should decline as more assets can be converted to cash.

Ideally, several factors should decrease the need for life insurance in later years. One is the fact that the surviving widow or widower will be able to pay estate taxes from a well-balanced estate. This includes a periodic review of the cost of dying, which is good planning.

By considering gifts to the work of God at the death of the survivor, taxes may be significantly reduced or entirely eliminated. This is good stewardship, but in the process be sure survivors' needs are adequately cared for. Trusts may be useful in accomplishing both purposes. (See chapters 5 and 11.) Elderly owners of estates should begin making living gifts to loved ones, thereby also reducing estate settlement costs.

Now, how much insurance is enough? Let's simply answer this from the perspective of protection in view of death. Life insurance salesmen often use a rule of thumb that you purchase five to seven times your annual income in life insurance. This is a simple enough approach and perhaps is adequate in many instances. However, it would be wiser to study the needs and base the estimate on the facts of each individual situation. We would want to do exactly what Jack and Betty have done in the previous chapter—begin with a tentative budget based upon what a widow would need and determine the resources there are to meet those needs. In Jack and Betty's example we could eliminate the college expenses, or increase Betty's earnings, or carry out a combination of these efforts. If Betty's proposed budget is reduced and its resources are accurate, the need which remained unresolved was $218 a month. If life insurance is the way Jack wants to meet this need for Betty, then this answers the question, How much insurance is enough? It would take $32,700 worth of additional life insurance to produce $218 a month, if it were invested to earn 8 percent. Simply determine how much you feel an investment could earn safely, such as 8 percent, and divide the annual need ($218 x 12) $2,616 by .08 which equals $32,700.

I do feel one satisfactory alternative to simply more life insurance is for the wife to pursue a career about the same time her youngest starts high school. She could arrange to receive professional training and still be at home each day when her youngest arrives home from school. Her training could be completed by the time her youngest graduates from high school, permitting her to have a meaningful income-producing career of her own.

Without answering all questions, we have followed a course of action which will lead to an answer to the question, How much life insurance is enough? There are many variables, lifestyles, philosophies, and unpredictable economic events to consider in reaching a positive conclusion.

What type of insurance will meet the objective? Remember, the objective in this analysis is protection. We mentioned that all insurance is protection, or protection combined with savings. So all insurance is protection or has a protection element.

There are three common forms of term insurance, which is pure protection and normally the least expensive form of protection. They are *level term, renewable term,* and *decreasing term.* Level term is a type of insurance in which the death benefit or face value remains constant for a specified period of time. Let's assume Jack, in our previous illustration, is forty-five. He may wish to buy $35,000 worth of level term insurance for twenty years until age sixty-five to meet the needs his wife may incur. Renewable term would also give Jack a constant life insurance coverage for a certain period of time, but the premium would be increased at intervals. In effect, he would be saying, I will buy it for one year and then cancel or continue. The company would be saying, As long as you renew we will not cancel or require another physical. You are guaranteed the right to keep the policy in force. Future premiums rise as you grow older but are stated in advance in the policy. A common renewable term is for one year. For example, Jack is forty-five and elects to have $35,000 in protection until age sixty-five. Here is how the two policies would compare:

Level term: $572.60 per year

                         x20 years

Total cost $11,452

Renewable term:

Age 46 - $219.10	Age 56 - $506.10
47 - $238.70	57 - $554.75
48 - $260.75	58 - $606.90
49 - $284.90	59 - $663.25
50 - $311.85	60 - $725.55
51 - $338.10	61 - $793.45
52 - $366.10	62 - $867.30
53 - $396.55	63 - $948.15
54 - $429.10	64 - $1,036.35
55 - $464.20	65 - $1,186.85
	$11,197.90

You will notice that over a twenty-year period the two total amounts are similar. However, you have invested more money early in the level term as compared to the renewable term. Also, if the estate's value increases, the need for insurance will decrease in later years. If, in fact, Jack's estate increases in value to the extent he feels he no longer needs the insurance, in ten years he would have spent only $3,309.25 for the renewable term; but the level term would have cost him $5,726.

Decreasing term is life insurance protection in which the death benefit is reduced, usually annually. It also covers a pre-planned period of time such as twenty years or to some specific age. For example, Jack, hoping his estate value will be increasing each year, elects to purchase a decreasing term policy to achieve his immediate objective of $35,000 additional coverage. It might look like this:

Cost of Decreasing Term Per Year
Coverage
Age 45 - $35,000
    50 - $32,500
    55 - $25,000
    60 - $16,500
    65 - $ 7,000
Annual premium of $265.30

There are variations of these three basic forms of protection.

In considering the purchase of life insurance, two riders (riders are additional benefits in the policy) worth considering are the *guaranteed insurability rider* and the *waiver of premium rider*. The guaranteed insurability rider should be purchased by those who believe that sometime in the future they will need additional insurance. This guarantees them that up to a certain date in the future they may purchase additional insurance with no medical questions asked. The waiver of premium rider means that in the event the policyholder is totally disabled, he need not pay the premium after, say, the first six months of disability. Each of these riders should be considered, but with an eye on their costs.

The final question is, *What company should I purchase insurance from?* Find a financially strong company with the lowest cost insurance.

Shopping is an old American pastime. Some enjoy it and succeed, others ignore it and leave the result to chance. When shopping we really should not look for the cheapest buy, nor the lowest cost, but the best value. Shopping for a good buy in term life insurance protection is far easier than finding the best buy in cash value insurance. A life is insured in a no-frills agreement, which says that upon the death of the insured the company will promptly pay the beneficiary the face value of the policy. That's it—no dividends or cash values to consider. If Company A will insure Jack's life for $35,000 at an annual premium of $572.60 and Company B will do so for $495.20, the choice is easy, provided Company B is financially sound. There is a way to find out how financially sound a company is. The A. M. Best Company of Oldwick, New Jersey, publishes a book entitled *Best's Insurance Reports, Life-Health Edition.* In this volume the A. M. Best Company analyzes over 1,200 life insurance companies and assigns a rating to them. They assign a policy-holder rating to each company of A+ and A (excellent), B+ (very good), B (good), C+ (fairly good), and C (fair). These ratings are based on all of the financial data submitted by the companies and are a reflection of their financial strength. Best does not rate a company until it has been in business at least five years. They include in their analysis a financial-size category and rate the company based on its strength within its own size classification. Most large libraries would have this volume available.

Herbert S. Denenburg, former Insurance Commissioner for the State of Pennsylvania, published a series of consumer-oriented booklets about life insurance. In one of his booklets, *Shopper's Guide to Term Life Insurance,* he included a list of insurance companies issuing term policies in Pennsylvania and their comparative costs. This kind of comparison can help you make an intelligent decision about the right company to buy from. Study which companies offer the lowest cost and check the A. M. Best guide to determine financial strength.

Sometimes when considering life insurance protection you become acquainted with a person who is an agent. You decide the amount you need and the type of policy you desire. You know the agent but know nothing about his company. Back to A. M. Best. Again the company may be checked out in regard to its financial strength. A comparison with two or three other companies' costs and financial strength should help you with the decision.

Before you buy insurance, rethink your objective. What is your purpose? For our purposes here it is primarily protection. Each purpose must be evaluated separately. How much insurance is enough? What kind of policy will offer the best value and accomplish the objective in the best way? Finally, what company affords me the best value? Before you buy insurance, answer these questions.

TEN
AFTER DEATH—TAXES

It is often said that only two things are certain in life—death and taxes! Every time we turn around, someone has another tax plan. Someone said the purpose of new tax laws is to create new ways to give more revenue to Uncle Sam.

The income tax is taken in graduated amounts from your income. The gift tax is levied on a transfer of property during your lifetime. An estate tax is imposed on transfers after you die. Most states, along with the federal government, impose income, gift, and some form of death tax. Each state has its own view of taxes and each differs from the others to some degree.

Let's think about some taxes you may face when disposing of your estate. One word of caution first. Many professional estate planners focus on saving taxes no matter what. It becomes their primary objective. I don't believe it should be first; rather, the people for whom all the planning takes place should be first. They are the object of the planning.

Sometimes it is better to pay taxes in order that loved ones will not be locked into irrevocable arrangements designed with the sole purpose of saving taxes. The objective is to distribute the estate God has entrusted to us in the manner most beneficial to those we are responsible for, and in the most economical way.

In recent years estate tax reform legislation has been enacted. The federal government has established what is known as "uniform federal estate and gift tax rates," which means lifetime transfers are taxed at the same rate as those made at death. For most people these transfer taxes will be decreased or eliminated. Living gifts are accumulated and added to death transfers to arrive at the tax which will be levied upon these transfers. Taxes on lifetime gifts are called gift taxes, and taxes on transfers after death are called estate taxes. A large amount of lifetime gifts are excluded before there are any tax considerations.

There is a $10,000 annual exclusion (or $20,000 for a married couple who jointly agree to make gifts of that nature) available to every individual. Mr. and Mrs. Woods, as a couple, could give their six nieces $20,000 each ($120,000) and not have to pay tax on those living gifts. Often older people who intend to make gifts to certain loved ones in their wills go ahead and experience the joy of giving now, and avoid the tax and cost of transferring the gifts through a probate procedure. Caution should be exercised, however, so that persons do not deprive themselves of too much too soon.

A new provision in the law now allows unlimited gift and estate tax marital deductions for transfers between spouses. In recent years the restrictions pertaining to gifts between spouses have been liberalized. However, it is essential that whether these are lifetime gifts or gifts created by your will, competent legal counsel should be sought to be sure your intentions are actually in your best interest. It may not always be the best course of action to avail yourself of the unlimited marital deduction features of these new laws, as the net tax effect may be greater.

Transferring property to a "joint tenancy" arrangement with another person may cause that transfer to be subject to gift tax. If when the husband dies, the surviving widow transfers the title to the house to, say, mother and son as joint tenants with rights of survivor, in anticipation that when she dies her son may simply take possession, her transfer is counted as a taxable gift made to her son of one-half the value of her home. This is not to say that such a transfer should be avoided. It may be a wise thing to do, depending on the circumstances. Similar situations arise with loved ones who open joint bank accounts. However, in most instances no gift is considered final until the joint tenant who did not contribute to the account makes a withdrawal. As you can readily see, there could be some significant lifetime gifts made to loved ones which would entirely avoid taxation. When transfers of property are made which exceed these exclusions, they need to be recorded and eventually may become subject to tax if they exceed certain minimum amounts.

The tax levied on the accumulated lifetime and death transfers begins with a rate of 18 percent on the first $10,000 and rises to 50 percent (effective 1985) on transfers which exceed $5 million. However, certain credits were established which eliminate or reduce taxes. In effect, smaller estates are not subject to any tax on their lifetime or death transfers. The 1981 act made provision to gradually increase the sizes of estates eligible for this credit as follows:

1982	$ 62,800
1983	79,300
1984	96,300
1985	121,800
1986	155,800
1987 and thereafter	192,800

Estates in 1982 whose taxable transfers amounted to less than $225,000 were not subject to this federal tax. In 1987 and the years following, the combination of lifetime and death transfers would have to exceed $600,000 to have a federal tax imposed.

For example: Mr. Davis, a bachelor, dies in 1987, leaving his entire estate, valued at $600,000, to his sister. According to the Unified Estate and Gift Tax Schedule, the tax due on a taxable estate of $600,000 would be $155,800 on $500,000 plus 37 percent of the excess over $500,000. It would look like this:

Tax on $500,000	$155,800
Tax on $100,000 (37%)	37,000
Total tentative tax	$192,800
Less unified tax credit	192,800
Federal estate tax due	—0—

Let's look at the tax implications for a couple, utilizing the unlimited marital deduction. Let's assume the gross estate is $950,000 in this illustration.

A person's *gross estate* is all the property he owns or has a right of ownership to when that person dies. When you deduct all the administrative expense, probate, funeral, debts, executor, and attorney's fees, you have the *adjusted gross estate*. For example, let's assume Mr. and Mrs. Edwards have an estate valued at $950,000 and Mr. Edwards dies in 1987, leaving everything to his wife and taking advantage of the unlimited marital deduction.

Gross estate	$950,000
Less final expenses	50,000
Adjusted gross estate	$900,000
Less maximum marital deduction	900,000
Taxable estate	—0—

Upon Mrs. Edwards' subsequent death, provided her estate value remained the same, the result would be as follows:

Adjusted gross estate	$900,000
Tentative Tax	$306,800
Less unified tax credit	192,800
Total tax	$114,000

Mr. and Mrs. Edwards need to be sure that their wills are properly drafted to qualify for the marital deduction. Wills that are properly drafted usually allow for a marital deduction not more than that absolutely needed to eliminate taxes on the estate of the first to die. This can save taxes in the estate of the surviving spouse.

By providing what is called a *non-marital trust* in their will, Mr. and Mrs. Edwards might have saved $114,000 in taxes. It would look like this:

1. At Mr. Edwards' death:
Estate value $900,000
                    (no tax)

To Mrs. Edwards tax-free as the marital deduction.
                    $600,000

To a non-marital trust. Income to Mrs. Edwards with limited access to principal.
$300,000
(Mr. Edwards' tax credit would eliminate any tax here.)

2. Mrs. Edwards dies:
Estate value
                    $600,000

$300,000
Passes tax-free to children.

Tentative tax
                    $192,800
Less unified tax credit
                    192,800
Total fed'l estate tax
                    —0—

By this simple illustration you can see that by taking the maximum marital deduction without regard to how it affects the taxation in the survivor's estate, there might have been a tax of as much as $114,000 as opposed to no tax at all.

Actually, wills may be drafted in a way which

allows the surviving spouse and the executor the opportunity to decide just which way will be most beneficial to the survivor. However, we come back to our earlier comment that needs of loved ones should be of first concern. Maybe the trust, which isolates part of Mrs. Edwards' assets, is not in her best interest. Maybe it is not the intention of the Edwardses to pass along such a large portion of their estate to their children. But I do think this illustrates an important consideration. Work out the financial consequences of whatever you have in mind. Be sure you are accomplishing your objective in the most economical way.

The many factors which interplay in planning an estate this complex point up the need to employ professional legal counsel. No matter what choice you make, make sure you see why a given plan has been worked out for you, and be sure you fully understand its consequences.

You would think our loving, kind Uncle Sam would be saddened enough by our passing simply to say good-bye without requiring another tax return. Actually, a federal estate tax return will not be required from 1987 on, unless our estate amounts to at least $600,000. This is true because with the unified tax credit of $192,800 for 1987, no tax would be due. When an estate is of sufficient value, a federal estate tax return is needed. Form #706 must be filed within nine months of the death, and all taxes must be paid at that time unless an extension is granted. Various schedules appear in the first few pages of this return, allowing adequate space to outline all of the assets of the estate. Two types of assets are worthy of more comment.

It is surprising how many people feel that life

insurance is not included in the estate of the deceased for tax purposes. It is part of the estate if the decedent owned the policy. Sometimes people feel it is wise to transfer ownership of life insurance policies on husbands' lives to their wives. This may or may not be wise, depending once again on the ultimate financial consequences to both estates. If it is pursued, it is important to seek legal advice in order to be sure the transfer is complete and the premiums are paid in a manner consistent with the intent desired. This can be particularly tricky in the community property states (Louisiana, California, Arizona, Nevada, Texas, Washington, Idaho, and New Mexico).

The second asset worthy of more comment is jointly-owned property. A brief look at property ownership may be helpful here. The two common forms of property ownership today are *tenancies in common* and *joint tenancies*. In the first type, Mr. Hart and Mr. Peterson might own an apartment complex as tenants in common, meaning that each has an undivided interest—normally one-half. Mr. Hart dies. Mr. Peterson does not own Mr. Hart's half as the surviving owner. Instead, Mr. Hart's heirs inherit one-half interest. The property at Mr. Hart's death might continue in a tenants-in-common arrangement with the heirs, or Mr. Hart's heirs might sell to Mr. Peterson.

Most people are familiar with joint tenancies because most residences are owned this way. It allows the surviving tenant or tenants to assume ownership of the deceased tenant's interest. This type of arrangement avoids a probate procedure. Some states have a "tenancy by the entirety" which is similar to joint tenancy. However, tenants by the entirety applies exclusively to a husband and wife.

Under the pre-1976 tax law, all jointly owned property had to be included in the estate of the first to die, unless the survivor could prove that he or she contributed to the value of the property in question. This is difficult to prove, and in many instances unwary families, not realizing that fifty years or so after they marry they must show how much the survivor contributed to avoid inclusion in the taxable estate, did not maintain records sufficient to do that. What happened then was that the total value of jointly-owned property was included in the estate of the first to die, then again in the estate of the survivor. But now when property is jointly owned by husband and wife with rights of survivorship, only one-half of the value of the jointly-owned property need be included in the estate of the first to die, regardless of the amount contributed by either joint tenant.

The remainder of the form #706 federal estate tax return asks for the details of lifetime gifts, funerals, debts, administrative costs, personal, and charitable bequests.

People who reach later years have a variety of attitudes regarding their assets. Some become insecure and withdraw, not wanting even to discuss what they own—I suppose out of fear that the listener will want to take their assets away. Some hoard all kinds of things, never disposing of any assets. Even cash is stored in private homes, perhaps in fear of a repeat of the 1929 depression. Others, knowing the end is in sight, wisely dispose of their estates. albeit carefully. The main precaution is to avoid depriving oneself too soon of too much so that one becomes dependent on his loved ones for food and shelter. This is not a good position to be in. In some instances, estates have been given away to, say, an only child, a daughter who the father and mother know will care for them if they are in need. But the daughter dies and has placed valuable family assets in joint ownership with her husband who, if not sympathetic, may not be as kind and thoughtful as his wife toward her parents.

For years people have struggled with how to leave their estates to their survivors free of tax. Last-minute deathbed transfers were commonplace until gift taxes were imposed and tax rates increased. Later Uncle Sam put another wrinkle in the works by imposing a so-called contemplation-of-death ruling. The contemplation-of-death rule was put into the Internal Revenue Code; it said, in effect, that anything you give away within three years of death is to be re-added to your estate for tax purposes. If you could prove, however, that the gift was made out of a living motive rather than in contemplation of your impending death, it would be excluded. Needless to say, this rule gave rise to a great many court cases. In a rare act of simplicity, the Tax Reform Act of 1976 stated that any gifts made during the three years immediately preceding one's death would be included in the estate regardless of the motive. This applied to gifts of more than $3,000, which was a favorable distinction over the previous law. The pre-1976 law stated that all gifts made within three years of death were to be included in the estate regardless of their value.

In 1981 this provision of the law was eliminated with a few exceptions. The planned strategy of giving one's estate away "carefully" to avoid taxes has merit, and under recent tax law is more advantageous than ever. To repeat, there is now no limit one can give to one's spouse either by will or during his/her lifetime, and it is free of all gift and estate taxes. Also, the amount which may be given tax-free to others is $10,000 per donee annually or $20,000 if a married couple joins in the gift. As you can see, a large amount of one's estate may be given away when and if it is desirable to do so.

A seldom-used approach in estate planning, one particularly well-suited to distributing resources within one's family, is the private annuity. An annuity is a fixed sum of money paid annually for life, or for some specified period of time. Essentially it is a predetermined return of principal and interest. Commercial annuities are commonly issued by life insurance companies. For example, Mr. Posegate, age sixty, has retired and does not want to manage all of his resources. He buys a commercial annuity from his life insurance company, and for each $1,425 he gives them he will receive $100 in annual income partially tax-free. The reason it is partially tax-free is that it is considered a return of Mr. Posegate's principal as well as interest earnings. There is a formula in the Internal Revenue Service's regulations which indicates how to determine what portion of his income is tax-free.

Mr. and Mrs. Asher own a small farm of 300 acres. They are ready to retire. Their son Jim is married and has a family. They live nearby and also farm. The Ashers need income but want Jim to have their farm when they die. They decide to deed Jim 290 of the 300 acres in exchange for a private annuity agreement. The senior Mr. and Mrs. Asher remain in their farmhouse, leaving that to Jim and his family in their will. The private annuity reads that

Jim is to pay his father and mother a fixed annual lifetime income equivalent to 6 percent of the value of the land. A recent appraisal valued the land at $500 an acre, so the aggregate value is (290 x $500) $145,000. The Ashers agree that Jim will pay them 6 percent of that value annually or $8,700 until both of the Ashers die.

Let's look at the results of that transaction. Most of the value of the farm is removed from the Ashers' estate and beyond the reach of taxes and probate. If the farm has appreciated, only a portion of the appreciation need be reported, and it is reported over an extended period of time. This keeps the farm in the family and provides Jim's father and mother with an income. If we assume Mr. and Mrs. Asher are both sixty-five, then the income they receive will be 58 percent tax-free. If hard times hit and the parents wish to give back some of the income to Jim, they may do so up to $20,000 per year tax-free or even give all of it back tax-free by giving additional sums to Jim's wife. Care must be taken to write the contract in a manner which reflects the true value of the land; otherwise it may be partially accounted as a gift which, if in addition to the exclusion, is subject to tax.

Federal estate tax laws are complicated. Periodically we hear the outcry to simplify tax laws, but each time a new law is passed, complications result. The average taxpayer can no longer decipher the intentions of the legislators who write the laws. It is imperative that individuals who have estates subject to taxation employ the services of expert professionals. Recent tax reform has introduced many new concepts.

When it comes to planning for loved ones left behind, the effect of taxes must be considered and considered carefully.

ELEVEN
HOW CHARITABLE ESTATE PLANNING HELPS YOU

During our lifetime we accumulate, enjoy, conserve, and finally distribute resources entrusted to us by our great God. We are reminded in Scripture that "Every good gift and every perfect gift is from above, and cometh down from the Father of lights, with whom is no variablesness, neither shadow of turning" (James 1:17). Sometimes we lose sight of God and focus in error on ourselves, attributing our genius, our creativity, our skill, and our financial resources to our own greatness. God reminded the Israelites, "Beware that thou forget not the Lord thy God. . . . And thou say in thine heart, My power and the might of mine hand hath gotten me this wealth. But thou shalt remember the Lord thy God: for it is he that giveth thee power to get wealth . . ." (Deuteronomy 8:11, 17, 18).

Indeed the source of all is our heavenly Father. Sometimes amid the crash of materialism in our society today we lose sight of the real purpose of it all. The resources are so in focus that we lose sight of God. We become guilty of what Timothy was instructed to warn the believers in his day not to do: "Charge them . . . [not to] trust in uncertain riches, but in the

living God, who giveth us richly all things to enjoy"
(1 Timothy 6:17). "For we brought nothing into this
world, and it is certain we can carry nothing out"
(1 Timothy 6:7). As good stewards we will want to
account for how we accumulate and manage and dispose of these resources entrusted to us.

As we obtain certain resources we become acutely
aware of the necessity to manage them with care, to
honor God with the firstfruits, and to use them for their
intended purpose—the care and keeping of dependent
loved ones. After all, the resources belong to him.

Most Christians give with a scripturally-based intent, wishing to further the work of God. We learn it is a
joy to give! The world is attuned to the economic
wisdom of giving; there is benefit derived, something
in return—it pays. It is the taxwise thing to do in our
economy. To the committed Christian the tax benefit is
of secondary importance behind the donative act,
which is motivated by love and devotion to Jesus
Christ. That's why, when tax legislation in the future
no longer benefits the taxpayer-donor, the Church of
Jesus Christ will not feel the effects as much as those
organizations without a Christian basis.

As it is now, federal and state governments encour-
age gifts to churches, mission agencies, hospitals,
schools, and other publicly supported charities by
allowing charitable deductions for gifts to these institutions. The tax benefits are worthwhile, and it is an
act of good stewardship to take advantage of them.
Inevitably the result is that the estate tax is lessened or
even eliminated because estates are smaller by virtue
of lifetime giving or gifts by our will.

There are many ways to give, although the vast
majority of donors simply give cash. Only recently
have charitable organizations begun to suggest to
their donors that they may give securities, real estate,
automobiles, equipment, antiques, art, something

from their farm or business, or for that matter anything of value. Uncle Sam specified, though, that if you give it you must give it with no strings attached. Real estate, I have discovered, is almost sacred to people. Most people would like their farm or home or land used for some worthy purpose, not sold to become just more funds for general ministry purposes. A unique feeling has developed for the family home or farm.

There can be some excellent advantages to be gained by gifts of things other than cash. For example, if Mr. and Mrs. Elliott want to give $10,000 to their church, they may decide to sell 1,000 shares of XXX stock valued at $10 per share to do that. They originally paid $4 a share for the stock, so they will have to pay a capital gains tax if they sell the stock first. But if they contribute the stock itself to their church, the church may then sell it and avoid the capital gains tax altogether. This is good stewardship. People need to know they can do this, and most of all *how* they can do it. I believe that most gifts like this are overlooked simply because people do not know how to do it or whom to ask. Here is the method most commonly used to make a gift of stock to the work of God:

1. Mail the unsigned stock certificates to your church or charitable organization. Have the post office insure them for full market value. Send them by registered mail and request a delivery receipt.
2. In a separate envelope mail a "Transfer of Stock Power" form signed by you (but not filled out) in the presence of your broker or banker to the organization at the same address. Your signature (or signatures if jointly owned) should be exactly as your name appears on the stock certificate.
3. Enclose a letter stating that the stock is a contribution to the church or organization and release all claim to it. Our broker tells us that this is important.

You can make outright gifts of almost any kind of property that has appreciated in value and gain this same benefit. It is an excellent tax-savings technique. How these gifts are deductible on your tax returns and to what extent they are deductible varies with the type of gift, the length of time you have owned it, in some instances how the church or organization intends to use it, and the type of organization or foundation you donate it to.

Outright gifts not only result in current income tax benefits, but also reduce estate taxes by reducing the value of the estate. A good example of this would be gifts of life insurance. Not uncommonly, people maintain insurance policies sometimes beyond their originally intended use.

For example, Mr. and Mrs. Hughes are sixty-five and retired. When Mr. Hughes began as an apprentice in the tire business, he purchased a $25,000 ordinary life policy which had cash value. He was, in a sense, establishing an estate for his wife while he was still young. As the years rolled by, he slowly built a thriving business of his own, creating a far greater estate. Recently he sold the business and is in a very favorable position financially. In fact, the last thing he needs just now is the life insurance policy, so he gives it to his church. By donating it to his church he moves it off the "top" of his estate and reduces his estate tax. He also receives an income tax deduction for the replacement value of the policy. If he still had premiums to be paid on it, his charitable deduction would be the policy's cash surrender value. He may choose to pay the premiums, which would generate additional income tax deductions for him, or let the church choose to cash it in or continue the premiums and keep the policy in force.

It may not be wise for certain people to give away the major share of their estate, even in retirement years. Many older people are property rich and income poor. Sometimes a person may feel he would like to give

away an asset which forms a major part of his estate;
but if he does, it will deplete his lifelong savings.
Let's assume a widow, age sixty-eight (we'll call her
Mrs. Hayes), has adequate income and a modest
amount of investments in securities. She would like
very much to donate her lovely home together with the
five acres of land. Her home is situated adjacent to a
Christian college. She is moving south to a warmer
climate. The appraised value of the home and land is
$125,000. There is no mortgage on the property. She
has been offered a residence in a retirement complex
for $65,000. She sells her home to the college for
$75,000, allowing some extra funds to pay capital
gains tax if the property has appreciated in value and
if she has previously used her "one-time" exemption
on the sale of property subject to capital gains. She
will have a charitable income tax deduction for the
difference between the sale price and fair market
value of the property. This is called a bargain sale. It
helps the college and helps Mrs. Hayes. It is a partial
gift and partial sale.

Let's assume Mrs. Hayes has adequate cash reserves
to buy her retirement home down south, but needs
additional income. Instead of selling her $125,000
property to the college, she gives it to the college,
subject to a gift annuity contract. While charitable
organizations normally are cautious about assuming
ownership of real property in exchange for an income,
the college desperately needs additional space and can
erect a dorm and enlarge their campus based on Mrs.
Hayes' gift. The college should have a reserve account
from which to make payments.

Let's look at the result. This annuity is quite similar
to the private annuity discussed in chapter 10. However, in this case the college uses the annuity payout
guidelines suggested by the Committee on Gift Annuities of New York, which recommends for Mrs. Hayes,

age sixty-eight, an annual annuity of 6.5 percent of $125,000, or $8,125 per year. Mrs. Hayes agrees to receive quarterly payments from the college. Her gift for income tax purposes will be $42,783. There is a Treasury Department table which sets a guideline to follow in calculating the value of her gift. The value of the gift is considered to be the amount the annuitant paid over and above what a commercial annuity would have cost for a similar annual income. So in essence the Treasury Department is saying that Mrs. Hayes could have gone to an insurance company and purchased an annuity for $82,217 that would have paid her $8,125 a year in income. So by transferring $125,000 to the college she has actually paid an additional $42,783 which is considered a gift. Had Mrs. Hayes given the college $125,000 in cash, the institution might have gone to an insurance company and purchased an annuity for Mrs. Hayes which theoretically would cost the school $82,217. The company would then be responsible to pay Mrs. Hayes each year and the school would keep the $42,873.

Had Mrs. Hayes sold her property, it would have been subject to capital gains tax if she had not used her one-time exemption. By transferring the property to an annuity, her capital gains will be smaller than if she had sold the property. In addition, the gain will be reported in equal installments over her life expectancy. From a tax standpoint, that is a most favorable treatment. In addition to her receiving an income tax deduction and favorable capital gains treatment, she would be removing the value of her home from her estate and eliminating the estate tax on its value. Of Mrs. Hayes' annual income of $8,125, $5,237 will be considered tax-free income.

I think a great many churches could take advantage of this approach. Recently a fast-growing church out west, located in a rapidly growing community, needed land on which to expand. The estimated building costs would stretch their faith and the land costs would add significantly to the whole project.

A widow in her seventies owned several hundred acres in the area the church thought to be a prime location. She did not wish to sell, as her capital gains tax would have been very high, but she could use the additional income which the sale would generate. She had a personal interest in the church and in the ministry. When the annuity concept was explained to her and her attorney, both agreed that this would be an excellent way to accomplish her objective and provide the church with the land they needed. Subsequently the land was appraised and transferred to the church. Based on the value of the land and the donor's life expectancy, an annual income (partially tax free) was agreed upon. The donor received a charitable contribution deduction for income tax purposes, removed this asset from the top of her estate tax bracket, and had her capital gains tax reduced significantly, as well as having payment of those capital gains spread over her life expectancy. One benefit to the church was that they received the land with a deed, free and clear of any liens or mortgage. The annuity does not constitute a lien or mortgage.

Sometimes you read an advertisement for gift annuities in a Christian periodical urging you to "invest" in a gift annuity. I don't think one should refer to an annuity as an investment. In fact, California expressly prohibits a reference to gift annuities as an "investment" in promotional literature. Even if a Christian organization could refer to them as investments, it would be far better to refer to them as gifts. A prospective donor should always check with the charitable organization he is interested in to be sure it is authorized to issue annuities in his state.

An annuity gives you a fixed return in exchange for

your gift. This simply means that you will know exactly what your dollar value will be in the future. The problem is you do not know what the value of the dollar will be! This makes an annuity especially vulnerable to erosion in value as a result of inflation. Perhaps you heard about the father who was teaching his son the value of the dollar. He did such a good job the little boy said, "Dad, I want my allowance from now on in Swiss francs!"

One friend of mine calls annuities a scientific return of principal and interest. Because they have a fixed return, they should probably not be obtained by younger people who need to experience growth in their estates.

One of the most popular charitable gift agreements was created by the Tax Reform Act of 1969. It is called a *charitable remainder unitrust.* The donor or donors transfer cash or assets to a trustee who, in turn, pays a beneficiary (or benficiaries), usually the donor, a fixed percentage, not less than 5 percent, of the trust assets as revalued annually. When the income beneficiary or beneficiaries die, the charity receives the remaining assets.

For example, Mr. and Mrs. Burke, age sixty, transfer $50,000 worth of corporate stock to a trustee, requesting a lifetime income based on 6 percent of the trust assets be paid to them.

Year One		Income Payment
Value of stock	$50,000	$3,000
Year Two		
Value of stock	$45,000	$2,700
Year Three		
Value of stock	$60,000	$3,600

... and so on.

Let's suppose, however, that they will not retire for five years, so they inform the trustee that growth might be a better objective now with a higher income benefit later. The Internal Revenue Code says the trustee need only pay the actual income if it is less than the agreed-upon percentage. Later deficiencies, then, may be made up. For example:

Year	Asset Value	2% Earnings	Paid to Income Beneficiary	6% of Value	Back Payments Due Beneficiary*	Accumulated Payments Due Beneficiary
One	$ 50,000	$1,000	$1,000	$3,000	$ 2,000	$ 2,000
Two	65,000	1,300	1,300	3,900	2,600	4,600
Three	80,000	1,600	1,600	4,800	3,200	7,800
Four	90,000	1,800	1,800	5,400	3,600	11,400
Five	100,000	2,000	2,000	6,000	4,000	15,400
		9% Earnings				
Six	100,000	9,000	9,000	6,000	−3,000	12,400
Seven	100,000	9,000	9,000	6,000	−3,000	9,400
Eight	100,000	9,000	9,000	6,000	−3,000	6,400
Nine	100,000	9,000	9,000	6,000	−3,000	3,400
Ten	100,000	9,000	9,000	6,000	−3,000	400
Eleven	102,600	9,000	6,400	6,156	−400	—

*6% of trust assets less actual payment

In this illustration the Burkes' trustee managed their stock in such a way that it increased in value from $50,000 to $100,000 in five years. (Not every trust will double in five years—some may go down.)

Their trust was written in a way that the trustee was not obligated to pay a full 6 percent of the trust assets annually, but only the actual earnings. As the Burkes retired, they looked to the trustee for more income. He moved their investment from a growth position to a high-income earning 9 percent return. The way the Burke trust was written, the trustee could not only now pay the full 6 percent of the trust value each year but also, since the trust was earning 9 percent, actually pay all of the earnings until the deficiencies were made up. After the tenth year the asset value will increase annually because it is earning 9 percent, all deficiencies are made up, and the trustee now only pays out 6 percent of the annual value. So in essence, the annual income will increase each year depending on the term and nature of the 9 percent earnings.

This trust provides the kind of flexibility more suited to our economy than a fixed income return will yield. Another enormous benefit of the charitable remainder unitrust is that if the donor transfers property subject to capital gains, there is no capital gains tax to pay when the trust eventually sells the property.

Here is another example: Mr. Edwin Carthage transfers a 100-acre parcel he has had for many years to the trustee of a charitable remainder unitrust. He paid $20,000 for the land. It is now worth $200,000. If he had not transferred it to a charitable remainder unitrust but instead sold it and invested the proceeds to obtain a retirement income, he would have had to pay a large capital gains tax. But suppose instead he transfers it to a charitable trust; they sell it and use the proceeds to obtain a retirement income for him. They pay no capital gains tax on the sale and would have nearly all of the proceeds to invest. There would be the cost of the sale in either event. But now Mr. Carthage has a higher income, and after he dies his church benefits in the same way it would have if he had sold the property. The differences, of course, are that now Mr. Carthage's personal income is higher, the church no doubt will receive more, and the assets are not subject to probate administration. Then too, his estate, if larger, would have had more estate tax to pay. He finds that the charitable remainder unitrust fits in with his total estate plan as reviewed with his attorney. So it becomes a tremendous tax-saver and excellent stewardship.

The income is taxed to the beneficiary in the same way that it is received by the trust—that is, when the trust receives dividends it is counted as ordinary income and as paid to the income beneficiary is taxed as ordinary income. All ordinary income for the year and any unreported ordinary income from past years must be reported first. Next, capital gains income and undistributed capital gains from previous years is reported. Third, other types of income, and fourth, tax-free principal which may be distributed to income beneficiaries are reported.

Another type of charitable trust in use is the *charitable remainder annuity trust,* which differs from the charitable remainder unitrust in only one important way. The income to be paid is based on a percentage of not less than 5 percent of the trust assets as valued on the day the trust was created. So in the previous illustration with Mr. and Mrs. Burke transferring $50,000 into an annuity trust of this nature, using their preselected rate of 6 percent, they would receive $3,000 annually regardless of trust earnings or fluctuations. So you can see that this trust appears to be like the gift annuity agreement in that the income is fixed—a desirable feature in a down economy and an undesirable feature in an up economy.

This brings up another matter. In the charitable remainder annuity trusts, the agreement is written to guarantee annual payments to you regardless of the trust's earnings. Should the fund be exhausted by withdrawals or poor earnings, the trustee's responsibility is terminated and the trust closed. The charity receives no final benefit and the income beneficiary has no more income. What happens is that the trust fund becomes a separate entity. As long as funds are available, payments continue. When funds are depleted, payments cease. For example, had the Burkes transferred $50,000 to an annuity trust and the trustee could not sustain earnings high enough to continue payments for their lifetime, the payments would eventually cease. However, had the Burkes, who we will assume wanted a fixed income, transferred $50,000 to a gift annuity agreement, the organization would guarantee payment to the Burkes for the duration of their lifetimes based on the financial strength of the entire organization's assets. While most Christian organizations wisely segregate (as required by some state laws) annuity funds and reinvest in a manner consistent with their payment demands, the payments do not cease with the exhaustion of the annuity fund should it be depleted. The organization, by its agreement, promises to continue the payments to the annuitant for life.

These are some of the ways, then, that living gifts to the Lord's work may be made, both by outright transfers or transfers subject to the donor's receiving income. In either instance one must be sure of God's will and carefully plan in such a way that loved ones are fully cared for first (1 Timothy 5:8 and Matthew 15:5, 6).

If doubts exist about the wisdom and timing of making large living gifts, consider gifts by will. Almost any of the above illustrations may be applied in will planning. You may wish to establish an annuity or trust in your will. Here again the timing and specific plan will need to be handled by an attorney skilled in estate planning.

Mr. and Mrs. Marston feel they are adequately provided for and have been retired now for five years. Mr. Marston is seventy-two and Mrs. Marston is seventy. They have been helping Mrs. Marston's sister Ella, a widow, age sixty. At the death of the survivor of Mr. and Mrs. Marston, they have instructed their executor to purchase a charitable gift annuity from Interior Missions in the amount of $50,000. The income will be paid to Ella for the rest of her life, with Interior Missions receiving the remainder of the fund upon Ella's death. Should Ella die before the Marstons, the $50,000 is to be an outright bequest to Interior Mis-

sions. A variety of ways could be found to use annuities
or trusts to finally benefit churches and charitable
organizations. The same creative initiative God has
given to build an estate may be used to distribute an
estate in a manner pleasing and honoring to our Lord.

Dr. Paul S. Rees of World Vision tells of a retired
corporate executive who frequently said, "I am going
to do something substantial for your church and its
missionary program." Dr. Rees relates, "His promise,
however, lacked one thing—execution. One morning
his housekeeper found the dear old bachelor dead in
bed. It was discovered that he died without making a
will. It was further discovered that among his assets
were $400,000 in government bonds. Most of it went
back to the government. He lived under the 'illusion of
immortality.' He had plenty of time to do for God's
Kingdom what he had in mind to do. Or so he
thought."

Carefully consider the many benefits of charitable
gifts in your estate distribution plans. It may be that
part of the way your house will be left in order will be by
returning some of the resources given to you by the
Source of all riches to further his work in the world
when you leave.

TWELVE
FINAL CHOICES

From the cradle to the grave life is one series of choices.
Some are easy, happy, and fun. Some are made with
reluctance and sadness. Joy and congratulations are
in order for the wife who announces she is going to
have a baby. Happiness surrounds the preparation—a
new room, clothes, furniture, showers, gifts, and books
about a new adventure for the new mother. Finally the
little bundle arrives. More joy, adjustments, and growth.
Life has still more meaning with this new relationship.
The Psalmist so eloquently said,

You made all the delicate, inner parts of my body, and knit
them together in my mother's womb. Thank you for
making me so wonderfully complex! It is amazing to think
about. Your workmanship is marvelous—and how well I
know it. You were there while I was being formed in utter
seclusion! You saw me before I was born and scheduled
each day of my life before I began to breathe. Every day
was recorded in your Book! (Psalm 139:13-16, The Living
Bible).

God was at work in the mother's womb. Every day of
our lives is so significant, including the last! Why?
Because everyone is created by the hand of God.

Recently I heard a minister speak of a Christian's unexpected death as a tragedy, which left me with the connotation that it was an ill-fated mistake. But in God's timing it was not a tragedy. It was the scheduled conclusion of an earthly pilgrimage and a welcoming home for one of his servants.

A recent memorial service in our church ushered out one of our members, Air Force Captain Richard Goodwin, in just this spirit. A private funeral and graveside service were conducted for family only. The church and other friends were then invited to a memorial service. Michael Tucker, pastor of Pulpit Rock Church of Colorado Springs, feels that three areas particularly enhance memorial services. First, the body is not present because the funeral and graveside service are over. This relieves some of the trauma experienced previously and allows the memorial service to have another emphasis. Secondly, personal testimonies about the person feature highlights from his life including love, humor, and human interest anecdotes, making it a more joyous occasion. Finally, Pastor Tucker feels the service should conclude with a refreshment time, specifically to let people begin the process of learning to communicate with the widow or surviving loved ones. I think it is an excellent adjustment time.

Death, then, is the ultimate victory, the end of the earthly cycle, the beginning of a heavenly cycle. Absent from this earthly body, we enter the presence of our Savior to live forever with him.

I opened a copy of an eastern newspaper recently to read about the wife who awoke to the groans of her husband, only to realize he was apparently having a heart attack. His earthly sojourn was ending. She called the ambulance and off to the hospital they went. The doctors could not revive him—he was dead. Many have never experienced the unfolding events that follow.

Ironically, almost every wife and prospective wife is familiar with the process of expecting and delivering a baby. Classes are held, literature is distributed by hospitals and doctors. But probably because, as Margaret Vermeer expressed in chapter 1, we are a death-denying society, few are familiar with the events surrounding death.

It begins when a final determination has been made that the person has died. A physician or coroner (depending on the circumstances of death) determines this and signs a death certificate. In the ensuing months it seems that at least two dozen copies of that certificate are needed. It becomes very important.

The next decision is whether a post-mortem (autopsy) examination should be made. Sometimes the state requires this to determine the exact cause of death, particularly in situations of uncertainty. Medical science, of course, always benefits from all studies of body organs. Some people give permission for the removal and study of certain body parts, while requesting that others be left untouched. Others decide in advance to donate certain organs. All states have passed the Uniform Anatomical Gift Act. George Fooshee, in his book *You Can Be Financially Free,* has a chapter entitled "Two Ways to Give After You Live." In it he outlines the procedures to follow if you wish to donate one or more of the transplantable organs.

"How are organs for transplantation obtained?"
They are donated by individuals like yourself, with the donations going into effect at the time of death.

"How can I become a donor?"
Sign the card in the presence of two witnesses who also sign. Then carry the card on your person at all times. You will note that the card offers several options:

(a) indicates that you contribute any needed organs or parts

(b) restricts the donation to the organs or parts you specify

(c) gives your entire body for anatomical study

"Is there an age requirement for donors?"
Yes. Anyone 18 years of age or over and of sound mind may become a donor by signing the card. An individual under 18 years of age may become a donor if either parent or a legal guardian gives consent.

"Do I have to register with some agency?"
No. Your signed and witnessed donor card is all that is needed.

"Do I have to mention the organ donation in my will?"
No. Your donor card is a kind of "pocket will" and is all you need. Mention it in your will if you wish. But obviously it's important to carry the card and also inform your family and physician to ensure their cooperation.

"Can I change my mind later?"
Yes. Simply tear up the card. Nothing else is necessary.

The State of Colorado uniform donor card looks like this:

STATE OF _____
COUNTY OF _____ } ss

I, _____, first being duly sworn, at least (18) years of age and of sound mind, hereby make this anatomical gift as indicated below to take effect immediately upon my death. The words and marks below indicate my desires:

I GIVE FOR PURPOSES OF TRANSPLANTATION, THERAPY, RESEARCH OR EDUCATION:

A. ☐ Any needed organ(s) or part(s) of my body.
B. ☐ Only the following organ(s) or part(s) of my body as specified below:

_____
_____
_____

C. ☐ My entire body for anatomical study if needed.

Limitations or special wishes, if any _____
_____
_____
_____
_____
_____
_____

I fully understand that the above anatomic gift (organ donation) will be void upon surrender of my driver's license to the Colorado Motor Vehicle Division, or by execution of the gift revocation on the reverse side of the 90 day temporary license or photo license.

Subscribed and sworn to before me this _____ day of
_____, 19_____ .
By _____
                              Name of Affiant
My commission expires (date): _____

_____
            Signature of Affiant (Licensee)
_____
     Drivers Examiner, Colorado Motor Vehicle Division
_____
                    Notary Public

Most post-mortem examinations done by the hospital will be done free of charge and within twenty-four hours of death. Some people do, of course, donate their entire bodies to medical schools for study. I know of a case in California where the donor had done this. The medical school had given the donor a phone number so that his survivor could notify the school, which would then dispatch a vehicle to pick up the body immediately. However, the survivor, in this instance, let a mortuary take the body to hold for the medical school. The mortuary embalmed the body and the medical school refused to accept it. Instructions in these instances have to be followed carefully. Normally most hospitals will cooperate by keeping bodies up to two days.

Following any post-mortem exam and organ donations, the mortuary personnel will come for the body and will want a full set of clothes as soon as possible. Most people provide what is known as their "Sunday best" (but not formal) including all underclothing and shoes.

Next on the agenda will be an appointment with the funeral director to arrange all the necessary details. The first information the director will want is family information for the obituary.

What kind of burial will be desired? It is so helpful if this kind of decision has been made in advance. Three types are commonly used today. The first is cremation which, strictly speaking, is not a burial but a destruction of the body by fire so that all that remains is ashes. Some Christians are offended by this approach. However, the Bible seems to show that burials were done according to the custom of the day rather than by a uniform method adopted for all time. Cremation has become popular for two reasons: first, it is less expensive. Second, it requires far less space, something which has become a problem with our burgeoning population. The question, then, is what to do with the ashes. The mortuary will dispose of them, or sometimes the deceased requests that they be scattered in a favorite place such as the mountains or ocean.

The second burial approach is a crypt or vault, which is used to store the body in a building. Finally, there is the customary ground storage in a grave. Some local ordinances are making ground burials expensive by requiring cement boxes in which a casket must be placed. It is important for those planning the funeral to know if this is required by law or just suggested by the funeral director as an option.

Once the burial decision is made, the funeral director will want to discuss the service. The deceased's survivor is ushered into a casket room where sample caskets are on display. In a sense it's like a furniture showroom. The best are up front for easier selection. The funeral director, like any businessman, has products and services to sell. He would like to sell the best. Most of these businessmen are ethical and will not take advantage of the bereaved's feelings at a time like this. This is a good place to mention that your minister is probably the best person to consult with respect to which funeral home and services to use, as he will know about any unethical practices and can warn against using mortuaries which may not be ethical in their dealings. Selecting a casket is not easy, especially at a time like this. I think it should be emphasized that modestly priced caskets will accomplish the same result and may be used in equally good taste.

The funeral director will provide certain standard services to accompany the cost of the casket, such as the use of one limousine to and from the chapel and burial site, the use of the chapel, basic music, and so on. Extra services such as additional limousines, more music, obituaries in additional newspapers will add on costs. *Be sure all costs are known in advance.* These days, in Colorado a total funeral done in good taste will cost between $1,500 and $2,000.

Someone should accompany a widow to assist with the decisions. Most ministers are available to do this if loved ones are unavailable. It will be necessary for him to coordinate his schedule with that of the funeral home in order to set up the service. Michael Tucker, pastor of Pulpit Rock Church of Colorado Springs, showed me the following service outline, which is rather typical of those he conducts:

Organ prelude
Solo
Congregational hymn
Obituary
Prayer
Message
Prayer
Solo

At the conclusion of the service people are invited to view the body. Customarily most people seem to want a last look at the deceased. However, I think it is important for the minister to give people the option to not feel they have to file past the casket. Another desirable option is that only the family view the body prior to the service and have the service with the casket closed. The casket may even be placed at the back of the church near the entrance, with the service itself a sort of memorial celebration not focused on the casket, but on the loved one's memory and glorious future with Christ. Still another option would provide that the body be available for viewing one day at the funeral home prior to the funeral, and then close the casket at the service itself.

Pastor Tucker, who for one year was hospital chaplain at Baylor University Hospital in Dallas, has conducted many funerals and feels it is important for the family, with the exception of very small children, to view the body. I know of a widow whose husband died in an accident. He was cared for by the mortuary and placed in a casket. It was never opened at any time before, during, or after the service. There can always be that lingering question whether he is really there. Viewing the body can help the loved ones face the reality of their loss.

Following the service at the chapel, most bereaved request a graveside service. It can be brief but very meaningful. Another option, perhaps even better, is to have a small private family service at the mortuary followed by a private graveside service. Then invite all of those interested to the church for a memorial service. This memorial service can be a joyous occasion celebrating the victory won and the memories that remain, in the spirit of the Goodwin service previously mentioned.

Another detail is well worth mentioning here with respect to the terminally ill. When you know someone has only a week or ten days to live, and you feel God is not going to intervene but is calling the loved one home, plan everything in advance. Meet with the funeral director, select the casket, write the obituary, choose the clothes to be used, work out all the details. For those keeping the long vigil with the terminally ill, there can be a great deal of anxiety and loss of sleep. When the end finally comes, physical and emotional exhaustion is normal. At this point it is a tremendous relief to be able to tell the nurse in attendance that everything is taken care of.

The final choices are as important as the beginning choices, but saying good-bye is never easy, no matter how you do it. How we say good-bye, how we walk away from our earthly pilgrimage, can affect a great many we leave behind. Let's do it right.

Let's leave our house in order.

THIRTEEN
SAY GOOD-BYE— CAREFULLY

Saying good-bye to those we love is seldom easy. The greatest factor in saying good-bye is the expected length of the time we will be apart. Racing out the front door to school or a job is easy. A departure for a week's business trip for the husband involves more for the ones left behind, but Friday is always in view and dad's return awaited. The World War II soldier on a troop transport, waving good-bye to loved ones at the ship's dock, was part of an emotion-filled scene. There was the uncertainty of "if" as well as "when" and in what condition he would return. Travel is exciting. People are coming and going all the time in our mobile society. I watch a lot of people saying good-bye, often tearfully.

Recently we had the privilege of having a Swiss exchange student living with us. It was her senior year of high school, and she chose to spend it in America away from her family. Our gregarious daughter, Kathi, was her classmate. They became lovingly close friends. Kathi was with Barbara when she invited Jesus into her life. There were lots of exciting moments like that in our year together. Our family became her family.

She became part of us. Finally the day in June came when Barbara would have to return to Switzerland. Switzerland was so far away. When would she be back? Good-bye was not easy. I went to the window at the airport to gaze outside, wondering what I could say when her boarding announcement would come. She came up to me and I turned to tell her good-bye. Nothing came out but tears. We hugged. She was gone minutes later.

I guess what really set the emotional tone of our parting more than anything else was the length of the separation we knew was ahead. When we say good-bye to someone we dearly love because he or she is entering the arms of Jesus, it is even more difficult. We know he or she is better off. We don't know when we will see our loved one again. Maybe down deep we lack the faith to believe we will! Uncertainty of the future and the loss of a loved one is unsurpassed in its effect on us emotionally and physically.

We need to be prepared to the best of our ability for the effect death will have on us personally. Let me suggest some guidelines:

Acknowledge that death is inevitable. Let's help to overcome what Margaret Vermeer observed accurately about our culture: "We are a death-denying society." The effect of this is that we refuse to plan for death and thus cause confusion for those we leave behind.

Be sure you are ready personally to die. Study it as a topic in the Bible. When you do, you will recognize death for what it is—victory! Knowing the biblical meaning of death will change your attitude and outlook on the subject. Teach your loved ones what you learn from the Bible about death too.

Prepare for death as if you were taking a trip. Be sure everyone knows how to manage in your absence. Use the contents of this book as a checklist to be sure your house is in order for those you love.

Saying good-bye will indeed not be easy, but how grateful those you leave behind will be if you say it carefully, having helped them to understand and prepare for it.

So say good-bye carefully. Leave your house in order.

BIBLIOGRAPHY

Barnes, John. *Who Will Get Your Money?* New York City: William Morrow & Company, Inc., 1972.

Belth, Joseph M. *Life Insurance: A Consumer's Handbook.* Bloomington, Indiana: Indiana University Press, 1973.

Brosterman, Robert. *The Complete Estate Planning Guide.* New York City: McGraw-Hill Book Company, 1977.

Caine, Lynn. *Widow.* New York City: Bantam Books, 1974.

Denenberg, Herbert S. *A Shopper's Guide to Straight Life Insurance.* Harrisburg, Pennsylvania: Pennsylvania Insurance Department, 1972.

Denenberg, Herbert S. *A Shopper's Guide to Term Life Insurance.* Harrisburg, Pennsylvania: Pennsylvania Insurance Department, 1972.

Fooshee, George, Jr. *You Can Be Financially Free.* Old Tappan, New Jersey: Fleming H. Revell Company, 1976.

Hardisty, George and Margaret. *Successful Financial Planning.* Old Tappan, New Jersey: Fleming H. Revell Company, 1978.

Kess, Sidney and Westlin, Bertil. *Estate Planning Guide.* Chicago, Illinois: Commerce Clearing House, 1977.

Lewis, Alfred Allan and Berns, Barrie, *Three Out of Four Wives.* New York City: Macmillan Publishing Company, Inc., 1975.

Marshall, Catherine. *To Live Again.* New York City: McGraw-Hill Book Company, 1957.

Newman, Joseph, ed. *Planning Your Financial Future.* Washington, D.C.: U. S. News & World Report Books, 1976.

Stephenson, Gilbert Thomas. *Estates and Trusts.* New York City: Appleton Century Crafts, 1965.

Teitell, Conrad, *Counsellor's Tax Guide to Charitable Contributions.* Old Greenwich, Connecticut, 1976.

GLOSSARY

Administrator/administratrix—The person appointed by the court to administer an estate, including collection of assets, payment of debts, and distribution of the remainder to the persons legally entitled.

Alternate—A person who may substitute for another, such as alternate executor.

Ancillary proceeding—A supplementary proceeding.

Beneficiary—One who is designated to receive a benefit.

Bond—An agreement by which the estate is insured against a financial loss with certain stated limits as a result of negligent performance by an executor or trustee.

Community property—The designation given to property a husband and wife acquire during their marriage in a community property state. An exception would be property one or the other acquires by inheritance during their marriage, not transferred into joint ownership.

Contest—A challenge as to the validity of a will.

Decedent—Deceased person.

Deed—A writing whereby title to realty is transferred.

Equity—The value in property which exceeds all encumbrances against the property.

Executor/executrix—The person nominated by the testator and approved by the court to administer an estate, including collection of assets, payment of debts, and distribution of the remainder to the persons legally entitled.

Fiduciary—A person or corporation who agrees to be entrusted with a duty to act primarily for the benefit of another.

Guardian—A person appointed and charged with the duty of taking care of another person who, because of age or infirmity, is considered incapable of administering his own affairs.

Inter-vivos—"Between the living," such as an inter-vivos trust, also known as a living trust, established between living persons.

Intestate—Without a valid will.

Joint-tenancy—A type of property ownership which is characterized by the right of surviving tenants to succeed to the ownership of the property. Joint-tenancy between husband and wife is often referred to as a "tenancy by the entirety."

Liquidity—The state of assets readily converted to cash.

Majority—The age at which, by law, a person is entitled to management of his own affairs and the enjoyment of civil rights, usually twenty-one.

Marital deduction—The amount which can be left at death to a spouse free of estate tax. The maximum marital deduction is 50 percent of the adjusted gross estate or $250,000, whichever is greater.

Marital deduction gift tax—The amount which can be transferred to a spouse free of gift tax. The first $100,000 is tax-free, the next $100,000 is fully taxable, and gifts in excess of $200,000 are 50 percent exempt from taxation.

Probate—The judicial act officially proving the validity of a will.

Testamentary—Pertaining to a will; derived from, founded on, or appointed by a will. Taking effect after the death of the person making the will.

Testator/testatrix—The male or female who makes the will.

Title insurance—An insurance policy whereby a person taking title to realty under a deed is indemnified against loss by reason of title defects, such as encumbrances, within certain stated limits.

Will—The directions of a testator regarding the final disposition of his or her estate.

APPENDIX 1

Memo to My Wife

To: _____

From:_____ Date_____

OUR WILL

Our will is located_____

The executor who is designated to carry out the provisions of our will is
_____ If_____ decline(s) or cannot
serve, the alternate is_____

Our attorney is_____ (phone: _____)
and should be consulted to assist you in settling any of the legal matters
you need help with.

In the event our estate is subject to estate tax, our accountant is _____
_____(phone:_____). Two other people (financial advisors) I
recommend to assist you with financial matters are _____
phone:_____ and_____ phone:_____

The main provisions of the will are:_____

_____

_____

_____

_____

TRUST

Our will includes/does not include a trust. The main provisions of the trust are:

Trustee:_____

Assets in the trust: _____

_____

_____

Beneficiaries: _____

_____

Terms:_____

_____

_____

BANKING

Our checking account is familiar to you. However, I talked with_____
_____ , our banker at the _____ Bank
(phone:_____) who told me the following information which
relates to our account in the event of my death:_____

_____

_____

_____

Our account number(s) are _____

_____

Information about other checking accounts and location of checkbooks:

_____

_____

Our bank statements and canceled checks may be found_____

_____

Similar information pertaining to our savings account(s) is as follows:

1 Account number:_____

Name of Savings Institution: _____

2. Account number: _____

Name of Savings Institution: _____

3 Account number:_____

Name of Savings Institution: _____

Our passbooks are located_____

_____

Special information relating to these accounts in the event of my death:

_____

_____

_____

_____

INSURANCE

At the end of this booklet is a list of the life insurance policies on my life. You will want to collect these proceeds as soon as possible to help with the expenses.

Call our agent_____ (phone:_____)
to help you or have your financial advisor or attorney help you with this. You may write the companies directly, enclosing a copy of the death certificates. Also included is a list of the life insurance policies on your life and the children's lives for your information. The policies on all of our lives are located:_____

The homeowners policy is with _____ Company
That policy (#_____) is located_____
The automobile insurance is with_____ (phone:_____)
The policy is located _____
Our medical insurance is with_____
The policy number is_____ and is located_____

INVESTMENTS

Our stock broker_____with
_____ Company
(address:_____ and
phone:_____) has given me a complete list of our stocks and bonds as of_____
which is attached. As you know, this list and values often change. Notify him of my passing so that he can change his records.

Title to the stocks and bonds is as follows: _____
_____
_____
_____

The actual certificates are located_____
_____

DOCUMENTS

The deed to our home is located _____
and it reads that we own it (nature of title) as _____

I feel the value is approximately $_____ The mortgage balance
is $_____. The files which pertain to the home such as cost of
purchase, improvements, original closing, etc. are marked_____
_____ and are located _____
I made an inventory of our household furnishings together with the
approximate values. That inventory is located_____
The attached photocopy shows the contents of my wallet. If I am killed in an
accident and the wallet is not recovered, you will want to notify the credit
card companies that the cards have been lost.
Just a reminder about our safe deposit box(es):
No.:_____ No.: _____
They are located _____
The key(s) is/are _____
All the birth certificates are located_____
Other important documents and their locations are as follows:
Automobile titles/registrations _____
Income tax returns _____
Keys_____
Military records _____
Naturalization/citizenship papers_____
Patents and copyrights _____
Title insurance _____
Veterans Administration information_____

YOUR BUDGET

Here is the summary of your budget as a widow which we planned together.
These figures will be changing from time to time as the children grow and
their needs develop.

Monthly Income	With S.S.	Without S.S.
1. Company benefits $		$
2. Social Security		
3. Investment income		
4. Your salary		
5. Other income		
Total Income $		$

MONTHLY EXPENSES

Mortgage or Rental (Insurance/Taxes too) $ _____
Utilities   _____
Household/Yard/Furnishings   _____
Food and Household   _____
Auto Expense (including insur./repair/license)   _____
Clothing & Personal Care   _____
Education   _____
Charitable Contributions   _____
Gifts & Allowances   _____
Medical & Dental   _____
Vacation & Recreation   _____
Life Insurance   _____
Miscellaneous   _____
Other   _____
      Total Expense $ _____

EXPLANATION OF INCOME BENEFITS

1 You will begin receiving company benefits
_____
If you have questions contact _____
_____Phone: _____
2 To receive Social Security benefits, you will need to go in person to the S.S. office located at _____
Take care of this promptly because if you delay you miss some benefits. Take with you:
a. My S.S. card
b. Death certificate from our doctor
c. Birth certificate for each of the children under 18 or those attending college under 22
d. Marriage certificate
e. Your birth certificate
3 You are/are not eligible for veterans benefits. To receive these benefits, do the following:
a. _____
b. _____
c. _____
d. _____
e. _____
4 Investment Income. Here are my suggestions on how to use insurance and other proceeds to produce income for you. Don't hesitate to consult your financial advisors about this.

I project the funds you will
have available to invest as follows:

Invest
as follows:

Projected
Income

Source   **Amount**

_____ $_____

_____ _____

_____ _____ _____

_____ _____ _____ $_____

_____ _____ _____

_____ _____ _____

Total $_____ _____ $_____

Less estimated
cost of estate
administration,
funeral, medical
and taxes $_____ _____

Net available for investment   _____ $_____

Total $_____Total projected investment
                                 income $_____

Just one comment about your personal employment income. The local
Social Security office has informed me that as of_____(date) you
are limited in your earnings to $_____monthly.
For every $2 you earn over that amount monthly your S.S. income will be
reduced by $1. For instance:
Your projected S.S. income with _____ children living at home
will be approximately $_____
You may earn an additional $_____
          Total personal earnings and S.S. $_____

If you elect to earn	Your S.S. will be	Total
$ _____	$ _____	$ _____
or $ _____	$ _____	$ _____

You may earn any amount from investment income. There is no limitation.

MY MILITARY HISTORY:
Service Number_____   Location of special papers:
Branch of Service_____   Document   Location
Length of Service _____ _____ _____
From_____To:_____ _____ _____
Rank_____ _____ _____
Contents of Safe Deposit Box: _____

_____
_____
_____
_____

OTHER REAL ESTATE WE OWN is as follows:

Description	Location	Nature of Title such as Joint-Ownership Tenants-in-Common	Mortgage Balance	Date of Purchase	Cost	Approximate Value

Total _____

The file where more information is
kept about this property is located _____   The deeds are located _____

OUR BUSINESS INTERESTS are summarized briefly as follows:
Business information: Proprietorship, Partnership, Corporation

Description	Share of Ownership	Date of Purchase	Cost	Value

The following persons will be able
to help you with the business matters:

_____ (name) _____ (phone)

Our financial advisor(s) and attorney are also available to help.

_____ (name) _____ (phone)

DEBTS OWED TO US

Description	Terms	Present Balance	Location of Document

SPECIAL INFORMATION
Children's Names & Addresses

Children's Names & Addresses	Age	S.S. Number

DEBTS WE OWE
Here is an explanation of some long-term obligations which are not a normal part of our monthly budget:

Description	Terms	Present Balance	Location of Document

FUNERAL INSTRUCTIONS
Funeral Home_____
Address_____
Phone _____
☐ 1 I direct that my body be used for medical purposes as follows: _____
_____

☐ 2 I request post-mortem examination be made if desirable.
☐ 3 I direct cremation of remains.
    ☐ No ashes to remain
    ☐ Disposition of ashes as follows:

_____

☐ 4 I request burial in the following manner:

_____
_____

Place of burial: _____
Address: _____
☐ 5 I wish memorial service with no casket present.
☐ 6 I desire a funeral with remains present:
    ☐ Closed casket   ☐ Open casket
    (Special information:) _____
☐ 7 Service:
    a. Church _____
    b. Clergyman_____
    c. Prelude_____
    d. Solo_____
    e. Hymns _____
    f. Special Scripture or poems _____
    g. Other instructions_____

_____

☐ 8 I request that memorial gifts be given to the following:
Church or organization _____
Address _____
Other Information:

_____
_____

Signed_____
Witnesses:

_____ Date_____
_____ Date_____
_____ Date_____

LIST OF INSURANCE POLICIES   Date_____

(Husband) Name and Address of Company and Local Agent	Policy Number	Face Value	Loan Balance which Will be Deducted	Approxi- mate Net Amount Due You
1. _____ _____ _____	_____	_____	_____	_____
2. _____ _____ _____	_____	_____	_____	_____
3. _____ _____ _____	_____	_____	_____	_____
4. _____ _____ _____	_____	_____	_____	_____
5. _____ _____ _____	_____	_____	_____	_____

LIST OF INSURANCE POLICIES   Date_____

(Wife and children) Name and Address of Company and Local Agent	Policy Number	Face Value	Loan Balance which Will be Deducted	Approxi- mate Net Amount Due You
1. _____ _____ _____	_____	_____	_____	_____
2. _____ _____ _____	_____	_____	_____	_____
3. _____ _____ _____	_____	_____	_____	_____
4. _____ _____ _____	_____	_____	_____	_____
5. _____ _____ _____	_____	_____	_____	_____

APPENDIX 2

Information for Your Attorney

FAMILY INFORMATION

Full Name_____

Other names by which you are known_____

Address_____

Telephone: Home_____Business_____

Date of Birth_____ Birthplace_____

Social Security Number_____

Marital Status: ___Single___Married ___Widowed ___Divorced ___Separated

Information on any previous marriages _____

_____

Full Name of Spouse _____

Address_____

Telephone: Home_____Business_____

Date of Birth_____Birthplace_____

Children and/or Other Dependents

NAME	ADDRESS	BIRTHDATE

FINANCIAL INFORMATION

List Real Estate You Own

Description	Location	Nature of Title Such as Joint-Ownership Tenants-in-Common	Date of Purchase	Cost	Approximate Value

Total_____

List Bank or Savings Accounts

TYPE (Checking or Savings)	NAME OF INSTITUTION	APPROXIMATE BALANCE
	Total_____

List Stocks, Bonds, Notes, Etc.

COMPANY	NUMBER OF SHARES	DATE OF PURCHASE	COST	APPROXIMATE VALUE
			Total_____

List Personal Property (Automobiles, Personal Effects, Jewelry, Art, Furniture, Etc.)

DESCRIPTION	LOCATION	DATE OF PURCHASE	COST	APPROXIMATE VALUE
			Total_____

Other Assets

	Total_____

List Your Obligations *(Notes, Mortgages, Trust Deeds, Etc.)*

DESCRIPTION	TERMS	PRESENT BALANCE
	Total_____	

Other Debts

DESCRIPTION	TERMS	PRESENT BALANCE
	Total_____	

Insurance Policies

COMPANY	TYPE OF POLICY	OWNER	BENEFICIARY	FACE VALUE	CASH VALUE
				Total_____	

Do you expect to receive an inheritance? Explain. _____

Explain Retirement, Pension, and Profit Sharing Benefits. _____

Annual Income: Salary $_____   Spouse $_____
Investment Income: $_____
Other Income: $_____   Supplementary Income Information ____

BUSINESS INFORMATION *(Proprietorship, Partnership, Corporation)*

DESCRIPTION	SHARE OF OWNERSHIP	DATE OF PURCHASE	COST	APPROXIMATE VALUE
			Total	

OTHER BUSINESS INFORMATION

Continuation Plan _____

Sale Plan _____

Other _____

Beneficiary Information *(Person or Charitable Organization to Receive Bequest)*

NAME	ADDRESS	DESCRIPTION OF BEQUEST

Executor Information: Name someone who can ably carry out the provisions of your will. Be sure to select an alternate in case your primary choice is unable to serve.

EXECUTOR	ALTERNATE
Name	Name
Street Address	Street Address
City State Zip	City State Zip

Guardian Information: Select the person(s) you would like to assume the responsibility for raising your children. Be sure to request their permission. Here again name an alternate.

GUARDIAN	ALTERNATE
Name	Name
Street Address	Street Address
City State Zip	City State Zip

Special instructions or questions for my attorney: _____

_____

_____

_____

_____

TRUST INFORMATION

Briefly explain what you would like this trust to accomplish for you.

_____

_____

_____

_____

_____

_____

_____

_____

TRUSTEE	ALTERNATE
Name	Name
Street Address	Street Address
City State Zip	City State Zip

BENEFICIARIES OF TRUST

Name	Name
Relationship Date of Birth	Relationship Date of Birth
Street Address	Street Address
City State Zip	City State Zip

Name

Relationship	Date of birth

Street Address

City	State	Zip

Name

Relationship	Date of Birth

Street Address

City	State	Zip

Name

Relationship	Date of Birth

Street Address

City	State	Zip

Name

Relationship	Date of Birth

Street Address

City	State	Zip

TERMS OF TRUST
General instructions: _____

_____

Instructions regarding termination of this trust: _____

_____

_____

_____

_____

_____

Income distribution as follows:
Name _____   _____
Name _____   _____
Name _____   _____
Name _____   _____
Name _____   _____
Name _____   _____

Principal distribution as follows:
Name _____   _____
Name _____   _____
Name _____   _____
Name _____   _____
Name _____   _____
Name _____   _____

TRUST PRINCIPAL
The following property is to be included in the trust:

INSURANCE POLICIES   AMOUNT

_____

_____

_____

Real Property (describe)

_____

_____

_____

_____

_____

Stocks (describe)

_____

_____

_____

_____

Other Property (describe)

_____

_____

_____

_____

_____

_____

TAX INFORMATION
Record of Taxable Gifts _____

_____

_____

_____

_____

Estate Tax _____

_____

_____

Charitable Giving Intentions _____

_____

_____

_____